CIVIL WAR CHRONICLES

DARING RAIDERS

CIVIL WAR CHRONICLES

DARING RAIDERS

David Phillips

MetroBooks

MetroBooks

An Imprint of Friedman/Fairfax Publishers

Library of Congress Cataloging-in-Publication Data

Phillips, David L.
    Daring raiders / by David L. Phillips
        p.   cm. — (The Civil War Chronicles)
    Includes index.
    ISBN 1-56799-553-5
    1. United States — History — Civil War, 1861–1865 — Commando
operations. 2. Raids (Military science)—History—19th century.
3. Reprisals—History—19th century. I. Title. II. Series: Civil
War Chronicles (MetroBooks (Firm))
    E470.P448 1998
    973.7'13— dc21   97-30541

Editors: Tony Burgess and Ann Kirby
Art Director: Kevin Ullrich
Photography Editor: Wendy Missan
Production Manager: Camille Lee

Color separations by Bright Arts Graphics (S) Pte Ltd
Printed in China by Leefung-Asco Printers Ltd.

10 9 8 7 6 5 4 3 2 1

For bulk purchases and special sales, please contact:
Friedman/Fairfax Publishers
Attention: Sales Department
15 West 26th Street
New York, NY 10010
(212) 685-6610 FAX (212) 685-1307

Visit our website:
http://www.metrobooks.com

DEDICATION

This book is dedicated to the memory of Henry Harrison Young, who served his country as a junior officer in the 2nd Rhode Island Infantry Regiment. Young fought bravely at Bull Run and other early battles as part of the Army of the Potomac. He later discovered his own talent for scouting deep inside enemy territory.

Long after the Civil War was over, Young was killed while on a secret mission for General Philip Sheridan along the Mexican border. Had he lived to see old age, and had his many exploits been better documented, Young would be recognized today as the originator of Special Forces. He remains a significant figure in the unwritten history of the United States, and should be remembered as the brave and gallant man that he was.

ACKNOWLEDGMENTS

This book benefitted from the help of several individuals who deserve my thanks. First, Harry Pugh, a recognized expert on Special Forces of all nations, provided advice and encouragement throughout the project. Second, Bob Keene designed and created special maps to explain the part topography played in both raids and battles. Third, my wife, Sue A. Phillips, provided calm encouragement and a safe haven without which this book would have been impossible to write.

CONTENTS

INTRODUCTION

*"Always mystify, mis-
lead, and surprise the
enemy if possible."*

—General Thomas J.

"Stonewall" Jackson

Much has been written about the myriad aspects of the Civil War, from the illustrious leaders and little-known players to the remarkable battles and inconsequential events, from the country's economic conditions and the delicate balance of power of the North and South that existed before the war to the bold actions of a few brave and zealous individuals who agitated an entire nation into bloody conflict. However, missing from many of our histories is an examination of a now-familiar tactic that had a profound impact on the war, on military strategy studies, and especially our understanding of violent political force to this day: the raid and reprisal attack. These strategic innovations forever changed the nature of war.

There were many raids and reprisal attacks that were conducted by both sides during the Civil War, and it would be impossible to document all of them in this single volume. This work will focus on representative raids—some entirely unknown to the general historian—that were ordered against specific targets. While army-size raids, such as Sherman's March to the Sea and Grant's earlier operations in the vicinity of Vicksburg, are great raids, these maneuvering armies are beyond the scope of this book.

Daring John Singleton Mosby had a quick temper and a great deal of courage that often got him in trouble before the war, but served him well as a guerrilla commander. He and most of his men lived within the region in which they operated, and so were able to obtain food, shelter, and information from the population, as well as out-maneuver enemy troops operating in unfamiliar territory.

Many of the famous raider attacks carried out in the Missouri region were planned and conducted without traditional military objectives in mind. These raids and reprisal operations, while frequently bloody, did little to attain the military objectives of either side. For this reason, these are also considered to be beyond the scope of this book.

Raids that were conducted with true military goals in the minds of those who planned them—rather than raids executed simply to destroy property—these are the subject of this examination. The raids found here were generally conducted by small groups of patriots who had an impact well beyond their numbers. For example, the raid that resulted in the capture of Harry Gilmor is perhaps as well planned a raid as has ever been attempted and deserves study in the military's war colleges. With this raid and the use of scouts, a new tactic—the utilization of special operations forces—entered American military strategy in an impressive way.

Here also are the raiders themselves—soldiers of fortune, zealots, pirates, murderers—all men of conviction who often used incredible violence to achieve their political goals. One of these raiders, John Brown, would become a nationally recognized personality and as great a hero to much of the population of the North as he was a villain in the South. Other raiders—like John Singleton Mosby—have become legends. Mosby's guerrilla operations enabled him to capture a Federal brigadier general from within his own Union camp, an act so daring that it was reported directly to President Lincoln.

Raids also encompassed the full theater of operations of the war at large. Noteworthy and included here are a few of the raids conducted by rail, some involving great train chases and hijackings of locomotives; maritime raids utilizing battleships at sea; cavalry raids struck with speed and accuracy deep into enemy territory; and land maneuvers accomplished with spies, co-conspirators, and legions of self-serving partisans.

Newspaper accounts of wartime events and the sketches that accompanied them were frequently inaccurate or misleading. In "Recapture of a Train from Mosby's Guerrillas," the Confederates are shown using muskets as they attempt to defend their booty. However, Mosby's men relied primarily on the new revolvers and shotguns, seldom using a saber, much less a long musket with a bayonet attached.

chapter 1

A POLITICAL EXTREMIST RAIDS HARPERS FERRY

Terrorists usually band in small and relatively weak groups that utilize random acts of repeatable violence against helpless (and sometimes only symbolic) targets to accomplish political goals that they have insufficient power to accomplish through traditional political or military means. John Brown and the members of his small group were able to effectively use such an approach in Kansas and later in Virginia to create a political atmosphere that served as a catalyst for the emergence of the American Civil War.

Brown was a singular figure who had been drawn to the cause of the Northern abolitionists who sought to free all of the nation's slaves—a goal he adhered to strictly once he had begun. This violent political extremist was eloquent in speech and tenacious in action once he had selected his course, and he was soon to become a hero. Brown knew that he could not lose as he set out: if he were successful and survived the initial actions, he could gain additional support for the continuation of his efforts, but if he were to lose he would become a martyr to the cause he had chosen. Curiously, he was to lose his life after a highly publicized state trial as he became a national hero to the Northerners. Equally curious, this political extremist risked and lost the lives of some of his sons for the cause he followed as zealously as any terrorist with conviction.

After developing an intense hatred of slavery and all things associated with it, John Brown embarked on a personal crusade against it. He had failed miserably at several attempted business ventures, but where he had missed the mark in business, he had managed to fulfill his goals within the abolitionist movement. After entering into abolitionist activities as early as 1846, Brown arrived in the territory of Kansas to join five of his sons in 1855.

A crisis was developing in the area—one that had been gathering momentum since the previous year, when the Nebraska Territory

> *"You had better, all of you people of the South, prepare yourselves for the settlement of this question. It must come up for settlement sooner than you are prepared for it, and the sooner you commence that preparation, the better for you. You may dispose of me very easily; I am nearly disposed of now; but this question is still to be settled—this Negro question, I mean."*
>
> *—John Brown*

Armed men on both sides of the Slavery issue in the new territory began to conduct reprisals, which were followed by counter-reprisals in a spiral of violent acts by extremists who would be labeled terrorists by today's standards. Such extreme bloodshed and violence gave rise to the appellation "Bleeding Kansas"

was preparing for statehood. The whole region was north of the old Missouri Compromise line, where slavery was automatically excluded by law. The region was expected to become two new states; since both would be in free territory, they would enter the Union as free states, which would upset the precarious balance within Congress. Southerners were also concerned that the entry of Kansas into the Union as a nonslave state would leave Missouri, a slave state, surrounded on three sides by territory into which slaves could easily escape and expect to be assisted by abolitionists. The loss of an expensive slave was a severe financial blow to the slaveowner, and there was a great public outcry in Missouri over the anticipated statehood of Kansas and the threat that it posed.

The Kansas-Nebraska Act of May 1854 was cleared through Congress, and the compromise over the entry of new states into the Union was eliminated as the radical elements on either side of the slavery issue began to take over the political processes of the nation. The trouble between the two sections that had been feared for so long was about to break into the open.

Congress had left the question of slavery in the new territory to the Kansas territorial legislature. This left the decision to the voters from the side who arrived in Kansas in the greatest numbers before the vote to form the legislature. Both groups began to encourage settlers from their side of the issue to move into Kansas, and as Missouri was immediately adjacent to the new territory, it should be no great surprise to learn that the proslavery forces crossed the border in large numbers from Missouri to vote. They won control of the new territory's legislature and began to lead the political processes as well.

New laws were rapidly enacted to protect the property of slaveowners. It quickly became a hanging offense to hide a fugitive slave. In addition, the victorious proslavery forces managed to expel the few Free State legislators who had managed to get elected. By the end of 1855, one of the antislavery settlers was killed in a dispute with a man who supported slavery. Angry Free State men assembled and soon burned the home of the man responsible for the killing, who had gone unpunished. Once the brutal series of attacks and reprisals was under way, the cycle of violence began in earnest.

Leaders of the Free State movement called for their supporters to assemble in Lawrence, a town controlled by antislavery men, and John Brown arrived as a volunteer to fight the Southerners. Open combat between the two factions was avoided, but by May 1856 "Border Ruffians"—as the proslavery forces were labeled in Northern newspapers—attacked Lawrence and destroyed newspapers, the Free State Hotel, and the home of the governor.

This anarchic attack resulted in angry denunciations by Northern congressmen, and in one speech in particular Senator Charles Sumner of Massachusetts angrily denounced the raid and slavery, and spoke harshly about an absent senator from South Carolina. The following day, Representative Preston Brooks of South Carolina walked up to Sumner and began to beat him with his cane for Sumner's vituperative remarks made the previous day.

It was the devastating attack of the Border Ruffians on Lawrence, combined with the lawless attack on Senator Sumner, that managed to provoke a heated response from John Brown and his closest supporters. Brown decided that a lesson had to be taught to the attackers and their supporters, and he decided to give them a demonstration that would not soon be forgotten.

Brown selected his targets carefully from a list of personal and legal opponents he had developed in the short time he had been residing in Kansas. His supporters began to prepare their weapons for a raid that would be soon glossed over by the Northern press and overshadowed by the larger events that were to come, but that served to foster an atmosphere of suspicion and fear between the two opposing sections for much of the remainder of the nineteenth century.

Within two days of the beating suffered by Sumner, John Brown and a small party of supporters made their way to the nearby home of James Doyle, a man who had expressed proslavery views. After forcing their way into Doyle's cabin, they shoved Doyle and two of his young sons outside. The raiders responded to the begging of Doyle's wife and allowed the youngest son, who was fourteen, to remain inside with her.

After leaving the cabin, Brown and his men hacked their three unarmed victims to death with swords. The skulls of the boys were split, the arms of one body were severed, and the gruesome reminders of the visit of John Brown and his allies were left lying on the lonely prairie. Brown had sent an unmistakable message—and challenge—for the proslavery forces to consider.

The raiders immediately left the Doyle farm to locate another victim. Soon they captured Allen Wilkinson, a member of the proslavery Kansas legislature, and hacked him to death as his wife stood nearby, helplessly pleading for the life of her husband.

Wilkinson's skull was also split open, and a fourth grim reminder of Brown's anger and politics was left dead.

The raiders were to make one more murderous visit, in the early morning darkness of May 25, 1856. Seeking a local proslavery saloonkeeper, they learned that their intended victim was away, but that his brother, Dutch Bill, was staying in the saloonkeeper's house for the night. Dutch Bill's skull was split and he was stabbed. In a final brutal act, one of the attackers severed one of the innocent man's hands.

An unbelievable series of acts along Potawatomi Creek in eastern Kansas had

PAGE 11: John Brown was born in Connecticut in 1800, and was raised in a household of passionate Calvinism, a faith determined to resist all forms of evil and wrongdoing. After failing at several business attempts, he joined his sons in Kansas in 1855. He had been drawn naturally toward abolitionist causes and as early as 1851 his violent tendencies began to express themselves. At one time he told friends that blacks should kill anyone trying to enforce the Fugitive Slave Act. Brown had made a choice that would occupy the remainder of his life—militant opposition to the institution of slavery. ABOVE: Once he became nationally recognized, Brown soon had the financial backing of prominent citizens in the North, his "Secret Six," who provided funds for organization, training, and a large future operation. These wealthy abolitionists paid for both muskets and the thousand pikes soon to be in use at Harpers Ferry.

occurred. Brown had been recognized by several of the survivors of the night of terror, and there was a general outcry in Kansas for his arrest and punishment. Unfortunately for those from both sides of the slavery issue who wanted to see justice served for the dreadful deeds of Brown and his party, nothing was done to apprehend him.

Equally unfortunate for the nation, the Eastern press chose to ignore the facts of this series of atrocities, and several newspapers began to claim that no murders had occurred at all. Northern newspapers began to shield Brown and some actually began to defend his actions. In addition to the snow job by the Northern press, a congressional committee investigating the killings managed to ignore the series of brutal murders, as did local legislators, and much of the North. The propaganda war surrounding Brown's actions further divided a strained nation.

Despite its unnecessary brutality, the slaughter of the five proslavery men, the Potawatomi Massacre, came to be viewed by much of the North as a noble act against an oppressive society that held human beings in bondage. One man's terrorist had become another man's hero.

The acts of Brown and his followers, however, were entirely without justification. Unarmed civilians had been gruesomely murdered to achieve political aims. Unfortunately, the Northern press and the antislavery majority in the congressional investigating committee contrived to shield Brown from either punishment or criticism. He succeeded beyond what were probably his own best expectations: John Brown won national attention for his violent crusade against slavery, and with the encouragement he received, Brown began to plan a second, more spectacular raid.

For a while, John Brown remained quiet and conducted no further operations against his hated enemies, the proslavery forces of Kansas, but he had not given up on his overall goal of freeing the slaves of the South. Realizing that he would need arms—and these would cost money—he began a series

OPPOSITE: Brown's ferocious opposition to slavery in Kansas culminated in August 1856, when he and a band of followers hacked several proslavery settlers to death. RIGHT: With the financial support of well-to-do abolitionists, Brown organized a group of twenty-two men— including a few African Americans and several of his own sons—with the intention of capturing Harpers Ferry, the location of one of the only two Federal arsenals in the entire country. His plan involved the capture of the arsenal, confiscation of muskets and ammunition, and escape into the nearby mountainous region, where he expected slaves to rally to him in large numbers to fight for their freedom.

Harpers Ferry, located at the junction of the Shenandoah and the Potomac rivers, lay within one of Virginia's deep valleys where abundant water power and inexpensive river and rail transportation had allowed small industries to develop and thrive. Brown—under the alias of Isaac Smith—relocated to a leased farm in the vicinity of the little town as final plans were developed for the attack.

of ambitious fund-raising trips to the Northeast. Wisely obtaining a letter of recommendation from the leader of the Free State movement in Kansas, Brown began an extended series of trips between the Midwest and the Northeast, primarily Boston, where

he met with most of the more prominent abolitionists of the country. He managed to visit Senator Charles Sumner, still recovering from the attack by South Carolina's Preston Brooks, and soon began to receive small sums of money from his various supporters.

Brown, four of his sons, and about a dozen followers began to prepare for future operations against slaveholders. He was able to use the money collected in the North to purchase arms and supplies for his men, and he obtained the services of Hugh Forbes, an

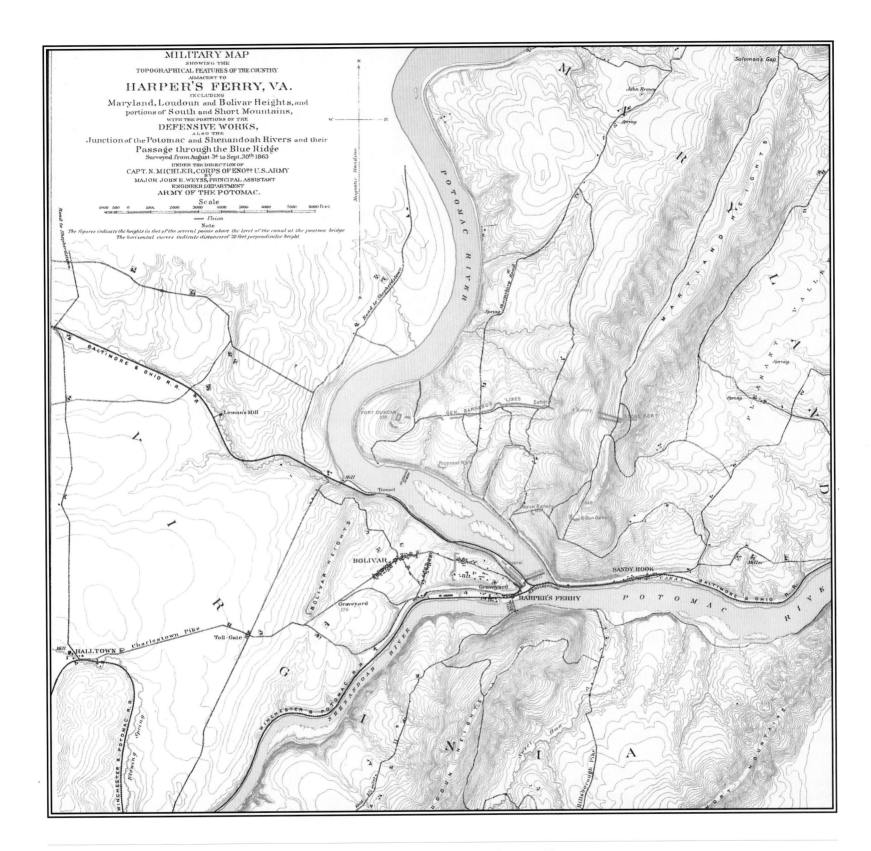

English mercenary, who was hired to train the small group. In addition to his supplies, Brown ordered one thousand pikes—long, heavy, archaic, spearlike weapons—but he didn't reveal his plans for these primitive weapons to anyone.

By May 1858, Brown was able to assemble a provisional constitutional convention for the United States that clearly stated his faction's intentions in its preamble:

Whereas slavery, throughout its entire existence in the United States, is none other than a most barbarous, unprovoked, and unjustifiable war of one portion of its citizens upon another portion.... Therefore, we, citizens of the United States and the oppressed people who...are declared to have no rights which the white man is bound to respect...ordain and establish for our-

selves the following provisional constitution and ordinances, the better to protect our persons, property, lives and liberties, and govern our actions.

Immediately afterward, Brown disbanded the convention, moved the Kansas men to Ohio, and sent John Cook of Connecticut to Harpers Ferry, Virginia, with orders to collect information on the town, its citizens—especially the slaves—and the layout of the surrounding countryside. The foundation for a major raid was being carefully prepared and Brown's supporters began to follow his instructions faithfully.

He had decided not to tell any of his financial backers of his specific plans, but he did inform Forbes that his initial operation would involve a raid on the U.S. arsenal at Harpers Ferry in an attempt to obtain modern firearms that could be used to arm slaves who would rally to his small insurrection. Forbes, unpaid by Brown, soon informed two abolitionist senators, Massachusetts' Henry Wilson and New York's William H. Seward (soon to be Lincoln's secretary of state), of the planned attack. Both kept the secret, but they were able to convince Brown's abolitionist supporters in the Northeast that they were involved in a scheme that had considerable personal risk for them. The Secret Six soon began to withdraw open support for Brown, but there is little doubt that they still hoped he would be able to strike an effective blow that would lead to freedom for the nation's slaves.

Well known throughout the country, Brown moved into the immediate vicinity of Harpers Ferry under an assumed name, Isaac Smith, and he rented the Kennedy farm in Maryland. Brown had quietly moved his base of operations to within five miles (8km) of the intended target. Some of his men remained in Chambersburg, Pennsylvania, where they received arms and supplies that

John Brown understood the fact that he could lose his life in the Harpers Ferry raid, but he also realized his very public death could serve to galvanize public opinion in the North against slavery as nothing else had done to this point in history.

were sent on to Brown in Maryland in smaller, less noticeable shipments.

On October 10, 1859, John Brown issued his "General Order No. 1," from his "Headquarters War Department, Provisional Army, Harpers Ferry," and, with his raiders, began to transfer the arms to a schoolhouse closer to town. At 11 P.M. on Sunday, October 16, John Brown ordered his small Provisional Army, composed of sixteen white men, four free blacks, and one escaped slave, to collect their arms and begin their long-planned "march to the Ferry."

It began with remarkable ease. Once the party of armed men crossed the covered bridge over the Potomac River, they entered Harpers Ferry, captured the night watchman at the arsenal, occupied Hall's Rifle Works, and abducted some of the more prosperous citizens of the region as hostages.

The forty-odd captives, including Colonel Lewis W. Washington, a relative of the nation's first president, were confined to a single room in the fire engine house at the arsenal where Brown had decided to develop his primary point of defense. His plan from that point depended upon the arrival of thousands of slaves, which he would lead into combat against their oppressors.

It was at this point that Brown's plan began to crumble. The slaves did not come; Brown, having no alternate plan, remained inactive as large forces were arrayed against him as the use of weapons revealed the presence of the Brown party.

An arriving train was halted and one of Brown's men fired at a railroad porter, mortally wounding him. Curiously, and as if a hidden hand were involved in managing this affair, the men who had come to save slaves had just killed a free black man. The townsmen, fully aroused by now, began to assemble with their firearms, and the raiders were forced to retreat into the arsenal buildings to escape the heated volley of bullets.

Once the presence of Brown and his raiding party was discovered by the townspeople, the men of the town and immediate vicinity took up arms to defend themselves. Their firepower forced Brown and his men to withdraw—taking with them several prominent citizens as hostages—into the relative safety of the engine house where they prepared to withstand a siege.

Drinking townsmen continued to fire at the raiders whenever an opportunity presented itself, and after several hours Brown lost his first man, Dangerfield Newby. A black man lost his life in his attempt to free others, but his noble sacrifice was unnoticed by the besieging forces as his body was dragged to a nearby gutter and left for hogs to consume.

Brown realized that he was trapped. He withdrew as many of his men as possible to the engine house, where he barricaded his party with his hostages and sent two men— one his son Watson—under a flag of truce to negotiate. Both were rapidly shot down, but the injured Watson was able to return to the relative safety of the improvised fort before dying. Soon another raider was killed as he attempted to flee, and three others were forced from Hall's. Two were killed; the third was captured and nearly lynched before he

was saved by a local doctor. The mayor of Harpers Ferry, Mr. F. Beckman, was killed in the free-for-all and the captive raider was murdered, his body used for target practice.

Local militia companies arrived and established a cordon around Brown's position from which there could be no escape. By sunset on the first day, a company from Winchester, Virginia, arrived, along with three additional companies of soldiers from Frederick, Maryland. Later in the evening, more companies arrived, this time from Baltimore, along with a small detachment of U.S. Marines. Two regular officers who were on leave from their regiments were ordered to take charge of the operation to subdue John Brown and his Provisional Army. Colonel Robert E. Lee, of the Second United States Cavalry, and Lieutenant J.E.B. Stuart, of the First United States Cavalry, had been sent to restore order and recapture the national armory.

Lee rapidly established order within the ranks of the volunteers and militia, even halting the Baltimore troops at a point nearby once the true numbers and condition of the raiders were known. Lee positioned the volunteers in a way that made any escape impossible and then waited for daylight before acting.

At dawn, Lee sent Stuart forward under a flag of truce with a written demand that Brown and his men surrender immediately and release their hostages, and that "if they will peaceably surrender themselves and restore the pillaged property, they shall be kept in safety to await the orders of the President…That if he is compelled to take them by force he cannot answer for their safety." Stuart was instructed to accept no counterproposal from Brown, who rejected Lee's terms. When Stuart signaled Brown's refusal, Lee ordered an immediate attack.

Lee sent a dozen marines under the command of Lieutenant J. Green into concealed positions near the engine house. Three of the men were equipped with sledgehammers to break down the doors of Brown's fort and begin the assault immediately. Lee ordered his men to attack using only bayonets in order to protect the lives of the hostages, but the initial assault failed to breach Brown's defenses; the raiders had placed the fire engine against the doors and tied them shut with heavy ropes. Lee next ordered his reserves to use a heavy ladder like a medieval battering ram to smash a portion of the door and gain entry.

Until now, Brown's firing had been harmless, but soon one marine, Private Quinn, was mortally wounded. The marines rapidly subdued Brown's surviving raiders, using bayonets to kill two who resisted, and Green struck Brown with the blunt edge of his sword after the abolitionist was pointed out to him by a hostage. The hostages and the slaves who had not participated in the fighting were soon released to return in safety to their homes. The active portion of John Brown's raid into Virginia was completed, but the political phase—the trial and the national publicity drawn to the infamous Brown—was just beginning.

Brown's raid was a small, timely spark, that when applied to the highly combustible mixture of fear and national politics, hastened the process toward conflict that in retrospect appears to have been inevitable. And he had one final goal: to become a martyr to his chosen cause.

The new Republican Party and its abolitionist members were quickly blamed for this raid by apprehensive Southerners. Virginia, in particular, had been sensitized to the effects of slave rebellion and had experienced the fear and terror of Nat Turner's rebellion, which left defenseless white civilians dead in the wake of black insurgency. Once the weapons collected by Brown—especially the cruel-looking pikes intended for the hands of escaped slaves to be used to kill their masters and their families—were displayed, a collective shudder went through Virginia. Accusations were directed toward the Republicans that suggested that the political party had plans to destroy the South in an enormous slave rebellion to be paid for by Northern interests. The fear of a slave rebellion and the hatred of the Republican Party for its suspected complicity in these acts would loom large when Abraham Lincoln won the next presidential election.

Brown was indicted for murder and treason in the regular session of the Circuit Court of Jefferson County, Virginia. His attacks, while on a federal installation, had violated state laws and his trial was swiftly under

Brown's men had securely barricaded themselves inside the engine house, but Lieutenant Green's men were able to use a fire ladder as a battering ram to smash through the doors to gain entry. Once inside, the marines were able to bring the hostage situation under control, even though they were ordered not to use their muskets, and had to face gunfire with only their bayonets.

way. Brown's intention to become a highly publicized martyr was soon to receive unexpected support from an unlikely quarter.

Virginia's governor, Henry A. Wise, arrived on the scene to take charge of this highly visible case and to use it for his own advancement. Wise, who had his sights set higher than the Virginia governor's mansion, hoped to transform the trial into a nationally recognized event that would provide publicity for him. Wise's interference with the events surrounding the trial played directly into Brown's own plans to promote himself as a sacrificial victim.

Brown won admiration even from his most unappeasable political foes as he revealed his total commitment to his goal. He desired martyrdom, and on the occasion of his sentencing (to death by hanging) gave a powerful speech that was widely read throughout the North. In part, the defiant abolitionist said:

> *Now, if it is deemed necessary that I should forfeit my life for the furtherance of the ends of justice, and mingle my blood further with the blood of my children and with the blood of millions in this slave country whose rights are disregarded by wicked, cruel, and unjust enactments, I say, let it be done.*

A powerful man had determined to lead the slaves to freedom or die in an attempt to draw supporters to his cause. His strong, eloquent speeches were widely distributed in both sections of the troubled country and resonated with a vastly different effect in each. In the North, he was recognized as a martyr to the teachings of the abolitionists, who were so greatly despised in the South; indeed, his name eventually became a part of a battle hymn that was sung as Northern soldiers invaded Southern territory to accomplish his goals.

Governor Wise, in anticipation of threatened attempts from Northern forces to mount a rescue of Brown from the Jefferson County jail where he awaited execution, ordered one thousand state troops to Charlestown to guard the execution. At least one member of the large contingent was moved by the historic event. Thomas Jonathan Jackson (soon to become known as "Stonewall" to the nation) wrote:

LEFT: Lieutenant James Ewell Brown Stuart, soon to be known as Jeb to friend and foe alike, was on leave from his regiment, the First United States Cavalry, when John Brown and his Provisional Army attacked at Harpers Ferry. Stuart was immediately recalled to duty and sent to assist Colonel Robert E. Lee—who was also home on leave—to subdue the insurrectionists.

Lee and Stuart swiftly gained control of the local volunteers and militia companies surrounding Brown and the engine house. Stuart was sent forward with an ultimatum from Lee demanding immediate surrender, but this was rejected and Brown sought to negotiate. On receiving a signal that Brown had refused to surrender, Lee ordered an immediate assault by a detachment of U.S. Marines. As Lieutenant Israel Green ran inside the engine house, one of Brown's hostages immediately pointed the leader of the raid out. Green had been ordered to avoid gunfire so that innocent hostages wouldn't be hurt accidentally, and he rushed Brown, beating him to the floor with the blunt surfaces of his sword.

...altogether it was an imposing but very solemn scene. I was much impressed with the thought that before me stood a man, in the full vigor of health, who must in a few moments enter eternity. I sent up the petition that he might be saved. Awful was the thought that in a few minutes [he would] receive the sentence, "Depart, ye wicked, into everlasting fire!" I hope that he was prepared to die, but I am doubtful.

John Brown walked toward the hangman's scaffold. He had no final words, but he passed a note to a guard in which he wrote that he was certain that "the crimes of this guilty land will never be purged away but with blood." He had worked long and hard, sacrificed several of his sons, and gave his own life for his beliefs.

The goal was admirable, though the methods he used hastened a national disaster, the greatest in U.S. history. Brown's use of terror to accomplish political goals served to galvanize much of the North, especially the new Republican Party, and abolition of slavery became a widely recognized goal. In the South, fear of political domination by Northern politicians and the simultaneous dread of additional raids designed to provoke slave rebellion created political unrest, which was capitalized upon by politicians with extreme views—such as secession.

The raid on Harpers Ferry by John Brown and his Provisional Army had far-reaching consequences for an entire nation.

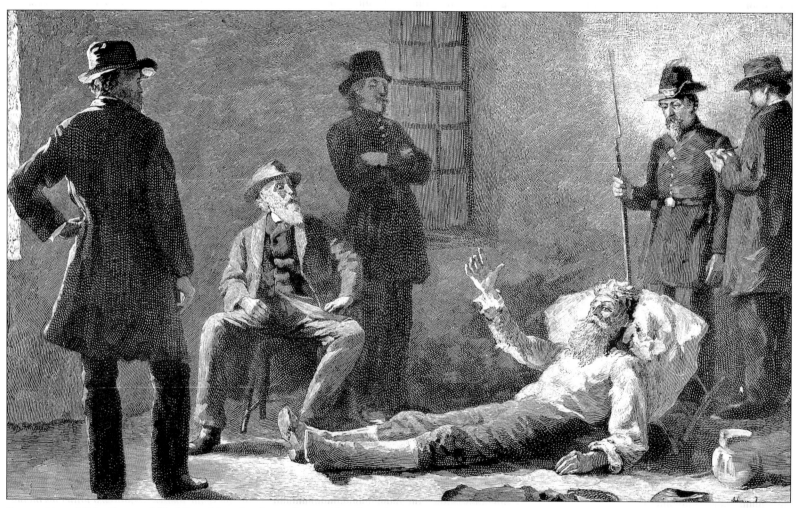

Once captured, John Brown shifted from his role of avenging angel to that of a persecuted Christian awaiting an unjust end at the hands of cruel tormentors. Brown brought the abolition movement to the front of national politics in a very dramatic fashion. He and one of his Northern backers, Thomas W. Higginson, agreed that his execution would do more for the success of their movement than his raid would have. The intense newspaper coverage of both raid and trial brought the issue of slavery and abolition to the attention of nearly every citizen in the country.

A POLITICAL EXTREMIST RAIDS HARPERS FERRY

"The result proves the plan was the attempt of a fanatic or madman, which could only end in failure; and its temporary success was owing to the panic and confusion he succeeded in creating by magnifying his numbers."

—*General Robert E. Lee*

John Brown's demeanor while awaiting his execution was selfless and rational. He understood his actual worth to the abolition movement, and said, "I am worth inconceivably more to hang than for any other purpose." His death resulted in the small, limited abolitionist effort becoming a general uprising of supporters in the North— many of whom would be wearing blue uniforms in a very few years as they prepared to invade the South.

A POLITICAL EXTREMIST RAIDS HARPERS FERRY

chapter

2

THE LOCOMOTIVE RAIDS

> *"The line that connects an army with its base of supplies is the heel of Achilles—its most vital and vulnerable point."*
>
> *—John Singleton Mosby*

Early on in the Civil War, both sides recognized that railroads were a decisive advantage to the side utilizing them most effectively. Northern and Southern strategists alike had been trained in the same academies with the same textbooks, and they had similar thoughts about warfare. Henry Wager Halleck, called "Old Brains" in the prewar national army, had translated from French the works of Henri de Jomini, a military strategist who served with Napoleon.

All the skilled officers of the period were familiar with the twin concepts of "interior lines" and "exterior lines," which referred to the distances to be traveled by troops seeking to reinforce a threatened section of defenses. Obviously, the side having to travel the shortest distance—possessing interior lines—had a distinct advantage over its adversary.

It became apparent rapidly that physical distances were less important to the general concept than was the time-to-distance ratio,

which could be shortened through the use of a more rapid means of transport. Railroads thus became a key factor in Civil War battles, and the side controlling the most rail mileage and rolling stock had a distinct advantage over the side lacking this modern form of transport. In this arena, the North had a clear advantage.

The Confederacy needed additional locomotives and cars for their railroads but lacked the industrial capability to manufacture them. Early in the war, the forward-looking General Thomas J. "Stonewall" Jackson developed a good plan to obtain a generous supply of locomotives from the nearby Baltimore and Ohio Railroad (B&O)—at the expense of the North.

Jackson had occupied Harpers Ferry, but he had not ordered any attacks on the railroads, despite the fact that there were many trains filled with coal being moved from the mines at Cumberland, Maryland, to the east-

"To move swiftly, strike vigorously, and secure all the fruits of victory, is the secret of successful war."

—General "Stonewall" Jackson, 1863

PAGE 25: The nation's railroads were generally composed of two vital components: the rails and the rolling stock that ran on them. These critical transportation elements were utilized effectively by both sides during the Civil War and were attacked as legitimate targets of war. The Confederacy had fewer railroad systems, and the Union army made frequent attempts to cripple the South's ability to deliver military supplies by destroying their railroads. Attacks were most common against the most precarious of the system's components, the railroad bridges. LEFT: Thomas J. Jackson, known as "Stonewall" to both sides after the Battle of Bull Run, managed a dramatic, but often forgotten raid on the Union's most crucial railroad, the Baltimore and Ohio, inside his native Virginia. Jackson was able to capture fifty-six locomotives, which were in short supply within the new Confederacy. Lacking rail connections with Southern railroads, Jackson ordered his men to use draft animals and their own muscles to pull the captured locomotives overland for nearly twenty miles, to where they were placed back on rails and sent off to support the Confederate war effort.

ern seaboard, where supplies were being stockpiled for possible emergency shortfalls in the future. There were double tracks on the B&O between Point of Rocks, Maryland, and Martinsburg, Virginia, a distance of some twenty-five to thirty miles (40 to 48km).

Jackson complained to Garrett, the president of the railroad, that the night trains were disturbing his troops as they tried to rest and requested that the eastbound trains be scheduled to pass Harpers Ferry between 11:00 A.M. and 1:00 P.M. Garrett, not wanting to be difficult with someone who had the power at hand to order his railroad blockaded, promptly agreed to this request. But since the empty cars were still sent back west at night, Jackson complained that it was just as noisy, and he asked that Garrett schedule his empty trains to pass on the double track during the same period. Garrett did as requested, and for a brief period each day the short distance between Point of Rocks and Martinsburg was filled with trains.

Jackson had created the perfect situation for a major train hijacking, perhaps the largest in history. As soon as his schedule was working and the rails were filled with trains, he ordered John Imboden to cross the Potomac River to the Maryland side and allow trains to pass freely until 12:00 P.M., noon, but Imboden was not to permit any additional eastbound trains to pass afterward. At that time, he was to destroy the rails.

Simultaneously, Jackson sent another force west to do the same at Martinsburg, catching all the trains that were going either east or west between these two obstructing forces. Jackson ordered all of the captured trains to be taken on the branch railroad to Winchester, Virginia, for safekeeping until additional arrangements could be made. Jackson had managed to collect fifty-six locomotives—more than three hundred cars—in a single hour.

As there were no additional rail connections south from Winchester, Jackson ordered

that his captured locomotives be hauled overland by horse and manpower from Winchester to the connecting rail line at nearby Strasburg. In a single crafty stroke, Jackson had simultaneously enriched the Confederacy's stock of locomotives and cars while nearly crippling the B&O for an extended period.

The railroads were used to great advantage in the war by both sides, and their value to military operations was quickly recognized. Defenders sought to protect their railroads as the attackers attempted to destroy rails and, whenever possible, the rolling stock that carried both men and supplies. The railroad systems became critical targets that had to be attacked or defended, depending on the perspective of the two armies. Control of strategic rails became crucial.

One of the more interesting but harebrained raids of the Civil War involved a strategic attack on a railroad that was believed to be critical to the successful

James J. Andrews, like Jackson a native of western Virginia, developed a bold and innovative plan to destroy one of the South's major railroad systems early in the Civil War. He and his Ohio volunteers commandeered an entire train while its passengers and crew were having breakfast. As nearby Confederate troops watched, the raiders took control of the train and ran it toward the North with the intention of burning strategic bridges along the route.

General Ormsby Mitchel was the Federal officer who approved Andrews' daring plan to raid along the entire railroad. Mitchel accompanied Andrews to several Union encampments as they sought volunteers for this dangerous mission.

defense of Chattanooga, Tennessee, in early April 1862. The Western and Atlantic Railroad was the connecting link between supply and recruit depots in the vicinity of Atlanta, Georgia, and Union commanders in Tennessee believed that Chattanooga would swiftly fall under their control if the railroad were rendered inoperable.

The entire operation arose from the suggestion of a courageous and seasoned part-time Union spy, James J. Andrews, who was very familiar with the area considered for the raid. Andrews, a Virginian, had made a number of trips into Confederate territory under the guise of a contraband smuggler. He had been able to pass as a dealer in medicines and other scarce supplies, thereby gaining the confidence of Southerners, and he had made more than one trip into Confederate-controlled Tennessee.

The Union army was moving south to the site of what would become known as the Battle of Shiloh. Andrews proposed a plan to facilitate the troop movements that involved destroying the railroad from Atlanta to Chattanooga. Once the line was inoperable, the Federal army could move forward without fear of encountering a coordinated response from the Confederates to the south.

Andrews and General Ormsby Mitchel visited the camp of several infantry regiments to request volunteers for this hazardous operation, and twenty-four men from the 2nd, 21st, and 33rd Ohio Infantry regiments volunteered in spite of the risks involved. They would be traveling in civilian clothing behind enemy lines. Exposure and capture would undoubtedly result in hanging by the Confederate authorities. All of the volunteers were enlisted men, except for one man: William Campbell. Campbell was a civilian who was in camp visiting his friend, Private Philip Shadrach, and when his friend stepped forward as a volunteer, Campbell also volunteered for the perilous raid.

James J. Andrews, the bold Union spy who conceived the dangerous raid along the railroad, had operated deep within the Confederacy on previous expeditions. Posing as a smuggler and war profiteer, the gentlemanly Andrews had been completely accepted by his unwitting acquaintances in the South. He was the last man they would have expected to be a Federal agent in their midst.

The men were divided into small groups with instructions to meet Andrews in Marietta, Georgia, on April 10. Three men were lost on the initial leg of the trip, but Andrews was able to assemble twenty-one raiders in Marietta on April 11. Andrews briefed them on the plan.

The volunteers were to purchase tickets on a northbound train from Marietta and wrest control from the railroad crew as they went along. The raiders would then burn the bridges they crossed as they rolled back toward Tennessee. Unfortunately for the plan, Andrews and his band saw more Confederate soldiers along the route than they had anticipated, and Andrews gave each man an opportunity to withdraw from the operation. They all agreed to proceed with the operation as planned, but two men didn't choose to make the rendezvous with the others to purchase tickets.

Andrews and nineteen raiders bought their tickets on the Western and Atlantic Railroad in Marietta at 5:00 A.M. the following day, and the raid was under way. The initial stop was at Big Shanty, seven miles (11km) from their starting point, where there was a breakfast stop. At Big Shanty the train's conductor, William C. Fuller, the engineer, Jeff Cain, and the rest of the passengers left the train. Andrews and his nineteen men remained aboard as the others left for their morning meal.

At about the same moment, Andrews ordered that the locomotive, tender, and three cars be uncoupled from the rest of the train. Privates Wilson Brown and William Knight, both engineers in their civilian occupations, climbed into the engine with another Union soldier to act as firemen. Curiously, they did all of this while being watched by Confederate soldiers camped beside the tracks, but the first realization that something unplanned was happening occurred when Fuller and Cain heard their train pulling swiftly away from Big Shanty. Andrews' raiders had succeeded in capturing the locomotive, the *General,* and the raiders raced toward the bridges that were their targets and the safety of Tennessee.

Unluckily, Andrews and the Ohio volunteers hadn't taken into consideration the courage and persistence of William C. Fuller and Jeff Cain. Initially, the two railroad men simply ran after the train on foot, but after the first few miles, they found a handcar and used it to follow the stolen train until they found an old locomotive, the *Yonah,* sitting on a siding.

Andrews' steps to ensure the success of his plan were almost perfect. He had ordered rails removed on the run from Big Shanty for

Andrews would have successfully completed his mission on the railroad if it hadn't been for the efforts of William Fuller, the train's conductor. Enraged by the theft of his train, Fuller pursued Andrews' men on foot, with a railroad pushcart, and aboard trains, forcing the Union raiders to push on without stopping to burn the bridges that would have effectively halted any further pursuit. As the chase continued, Andrews and his men were forced to abandon their engine, the General, and attempt to escape on foot.

the first twenty miles (32km) to Kingston, and he cut the telegraph wires. Once he had done all this, he felt that pursuit would be unlikely. But he made a fatal miscalculation when he passed the *Yonah* without stopping to disable it.

Fuller had encountered southbound freight trains in the vicinity of Kingston and was forced to abandon the old *Yonah,* but he ran along the track until he was able to locate another locomotive, the *William R. Smith.* Another break in the tracks halted Fuller, but he again dismounted from the train to run an additional three miles (5km) until he was able to board another train

The Great Railroad Adventure
April 12, 1862

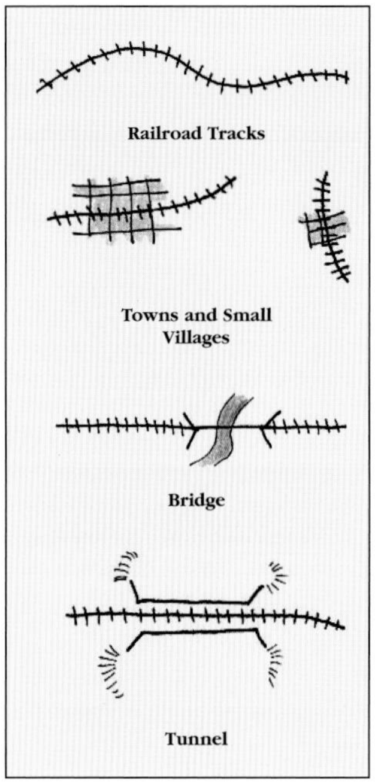

Railroad Tracks
Towns and Small Villages
Bridge
Tunnel

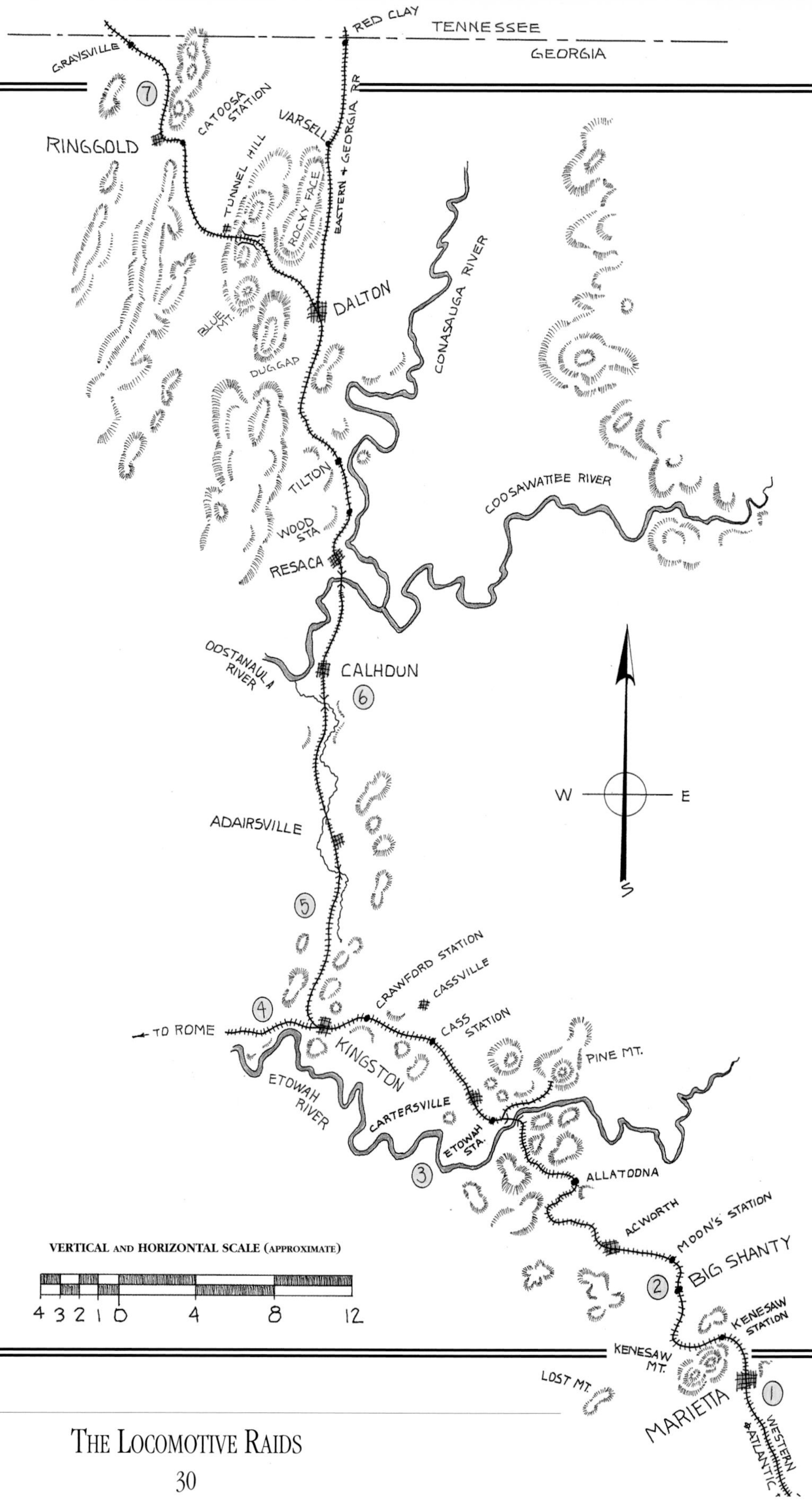

TENNESSEE
GEORGIA
RED CLAY
GRAYSVILLE
7
CATOOSA STATION
VARSELL
EASTERN + GEORGIA RR
RINGGOLD
TUNNEL HILL
ROCKY FACE
DALTON
BLUE MT.
DUG GAP
CONASAUGA RIVER
COOSAWATTEE RIVER
TILTON
WOOD STA
RESACA
OOSTANAULA RIVER
CALHOUN
6
W
E
S
ADAIRSVILLE
5
CRANFORD STATION
CASSVILLE
4
TO ROME
KINGSTON
CASS STATION
PINE MT.
ETOWAH RIVER
CARTERSVILLE
ETOWAH STA.
3
ALLATOONA
ACWORTH
MOON'S STATION
BIG SHANTY
2
KENESAW STATION
KENESAW MT.
LOST MT.
MARIETTA
1
WESTERN & ATLANTIC
VERTICAL AND HORIZONTAL SCALE (APPROXIMATE)
4 3 2 1 0 4 8 12

1. On April 12, 1862, James Andrews and eighteen volunteers from the 2nd, 21st, and 33rd Ohio Infantry and one civilian volunteer, boarded the *General,* a northbound train, in Marietta, Georgia. Their goal was to take control of the train and destroy track and bridges while en route to Tennessee.

2. At Big Shanty, when the crew and other passengers stopped for breakfast, Andrews and his men took control. Under the eyes of Confederate soldiers camped along the track, they uncoupled all but three cars and took off. The *General's* conductor, William Fuller, and several others started after the raiders on foot. Along the way they found a push car, which they used until they reached Etowah Station.

3. At Etowah Station Fuller commandeered the *Yonah,* which was working on a side track. The *Yonah* was used to pursue Andrews as far as Kingston.

4. The Raiders had blocked the tracks at the Kingston yard. Undaunted, Fuller's party continued on foot until they came across the *William R. Smith,* which had just come from Rome, and continued the pursuit.

5. Six miles north of Kingston the raiders removed a rail from the track. Forced to abandon the *William R. Smith,* Fuller and his party set out again on foot. Two miles south of Adairsville, Fuller's footsore group intercepted the southbound *Texas.* Running her in reverse, they renewed the chase. Andrews had encountered the *Texas* at Adairsville and had argued her onto a side track under the guise that they were a "special" loaded with powder for General Beauregard, so that he could pass.

6. At the village of Calhoun, ten soldiers from the 1st Georgia Volunteers joined the chase.

7. About two miles north of Ringgold, water and wood ran out and the *General* lost steam. The raiders, one by one, dropped off the train and ran into the forest. Five miles from Tennessee the *General* was abandoned.

Within a week all the raiders were captured. Andrews and seven others were hanged. The others were later exchanged. The survivors from this raid, all enlisted men, were the first to be awarded the newly authorized Congressional Medal of Honor.

Conductor William Fuller followed Andrews' men on a construction pushcart that had been used by men repairing the rails. Pressing it into use, Fuller and his men, including the train's engineer, continued their chase until derailed. Andrews had ordered his men to break the rails at strategic but inconspicuous points, such as on curves, in an effort to slow any pursuers.

pulled by the *Texas.* Once Fuller had abandoned the *Texas'* cars on a siding, he ran the locomotive in reverse as he chased the raiders aboard the *General.* The tenacious Conductor Fuller was soon closing in on the Union raiders, who were racing for their lives as the *Texas* and the *General* engaged in what has become known as the Great Locomotive Chase.

As the Union soldiers dropped cross ties onto the rails in front of Fuller's locomotive, halting him only momentarily, it became obvious that they would be unable to return to the safety of Tennessee, and one by one the men began to drop off the train to run into the nearby forest. With their supply of wood and water needed to power the locomotive dwindling, Andrews and the last of the raiders abandoned the *General* five miles (8km) from the Tennessee border.

Conductor William C. Fuller disrupted the Union sabotage mission when he undertook his personal pursuit of the men who had robbed him of his train. The operation was a complete failure. Within a week, all of Andrews' raiders were in Confederate custody and imprisoned. James J. Andrews was tried as a spy and executed by hanging in Atlanta on June 7, 1862. On June 18, another seven of the raiders were hanged—including Private Phillip Shadrach and his civilian friend, William Campbell. The two men who had declined to board the *General* at the last moment in Marietta were also captured, and fourteen of the original twenty-two raiders remained in Confederate prisons.

The Confederate authorities underestimated their prisoners, who managed a daring escape in October. Eight of the men evaded capture: four were able to reach Tennessee; two others made their escape to Federal territory in Mississippi; and two more reached the safety of the Union navy that was blockading the Gulf Coast. The remaining six were recaptured quickly and held until they were exchanged for Confederates held in Federal prisons. These brave raiders were awarded the new medal that had been authorized by Congress for military heroism, the Congressional Medal of Honor. Curiously, the highly regarded medals were awarded to men who were on an espionage operation in civilian clothing.

Andrews and Campbell, the two civilians, were hanged and received no decorations for their hazardous service and sacrifice. Nor was Private Shadrach awarded the medal—he had enlisted, had served, and was hanged under an assumed name.

The raid was well conceived and boldly executed, and would have served as a model for future raids along the line had it not been disrupted by the valiant efforts of Conductor William C. Fuller. It was entirely due to his remarkable tenacity that the Union's brazen

ABOVE: Once they were out of both wood and the water needed to develop steam for their engine, Andrews' men were forced to abandon the train and flee into nearby Tennessee. Within a week, all of the raiders would be captured and placed in Confederate prisons. Andrews and seven of his volunteers would eventually be hanged as spies. RIGHT: The Confederate locomotive General *was brazenly stolen by Andrews and used to withdraw toward Union lines along the Tennessee border. During their bold raid, Andrews' men traversed most of the length of the Western and Atlantic Railroad, but the tenacious pursuit of Conductor Fuller prevented them from completing their mission, the destruction of the crucial bridges along the route they were using to escape. Fuller's grit doomed the raid to failure, and resulted in the execution of eight of the brave raiders.*

raid deep into the interior of the Confederacy was thwarted.

The hastily conceived plan had no contingency provisions to allow for the unexpected—like Fuller's pursuit and the increased number of soldiers along the route. The Union army learned from this devastating failure, and rash operations like Andrews' raid would not be repeated in any such amateurish fashion.

chapter 3

AVERELL'S DECEMBER RAID

> *"I would define true courage to be a perfect sensibility of the measure of danger, and a mental willingness to incur it."*
>
> —*General William T. Sherman*

The Union army made many errors in strategy and execution of plans during the first two years of the Civil War, and as a result were able to claim relatively few victories. Perhaps it was due solely to an unknown source of inner courage and morale that the Union soldiers remained in the field and the Northern population continued to support their efforts despite their grim losses. The Confederacy had done remarkably well with its limited resources up to this point in the war, but the Union army was rapidly sorting out poorly qualified officers and replacing them with men who knew how—and were willing—to fight.

Operations continued against railroads and the supply depots and camps that were frequently associated with the rail lines. These raids, like the operation that resulted in the Great Locomotive Chase, were planned to accomplish more than simply the destruction of military property and an increased cost of continuing operations.

It was just this type of operation that developed in the mountains of West Virginia in December 1863, just after the region had entered the Union as a new state. This raid, like most of the others, had more than a local significance, but deserves a special place in history as one of the best planned, best executed, and most successful raids of the Civil War.

Following the battle of Gettysburg, Confederate General James Longstreet and his divisions were sent into Tennessee, where they proceeded to lay seige to the Federal garrison in the city of Knoxville. The garrison, under the command of Ambrose E. Burnside, was hard pressed and in danger of being forced to surrender.

Longstreet was receiving much of his supplies over the Virginia and Tennessee Railroad, which wound through the hills of southwest Virginia before entering Tennessee, and Federal tacticians felt that a raid against this vital supply artery could

result in a general weakening of the Confederate besiegers of Knoxville and relieve some of the pressure on Burnside before he collapsed. All of this was occurring at a time when the Union army was beginning to shift over to the offensive operations planned for 1864, and a Federal setback in Tennessee could easily have tilted the military initiative back in favor of the Confederacy and prolonged the war.

Brigadier General William W. Averell was positioned in northwestern West Virginia at a position providing some additional security to the exposed Baltimore and Ohio Railroad. He had recently completed the training and refitting of three West Virginia mounted infantry regiments and formed the 4th Separate Brigade. Having inherited his command from General Robert H. Milroy, Averell drilled his new corps until he was satisfied with its performance.

Averell and his troops, a single brigade of mounted infantry, were directed to cut the Virginia and Tennessee Railroad at some vulnerable point and interrupt the transport of troops and supplies between Richmond and

PAGE 35: William Woods Averell was appointed to West Point in 1851 and as an early army assignment served in New Mexico territory, where he gained practical experience in the art of the cavalryman. Soon to be a cavalry commander in the Union army, Averell fought his former classmates at Bull Run, and alongside McClellan during the Peninsula Campaign. He later took command of several regiments of mounted infantrymen in West Virginia, which he refitted, trained, and drilled to create the 4th Separate Brigade. With these men, Averell conducted brilliant raids deep within Confederate territory. LEFT: General James Longstreet, one of Lee's commanders at the Battle of Gettysburg, had been sent into the western theater as the East settled into a general lull following the Confederate defeat in Pennsylvania. After fighting at Chickamauga, Longstreet was sent by Braxton Bragg to besiege the Union's Ambrose Burnside at Knoxville.

Knoxville. Averell was unambiguously ordered to accomplish this assignment despite the obvious risks to the men of his command. The situation in Knoxville was judged to be sufficiently critical to justify a dangerous midwinter raiding party against the Confederate railroad. Although General William Tecumseh Sherman was able to raise the siege on December 3, 1863, Averell's raid was allowed to go forward in an attempt to further deflate the Confederate advantage.

Averell met with the department commander, Brigadier General Benjamin F. Kelley, at department headquarters in Cumberland, Maryland, where Averell devised an excellent plan that called for deception at every turn.

First, E.P. Scammon's brigade in the Kanawha Valley would move eastward to occupy Lewisburg on December 12. Scammon and his troops would remain in position until December 18, but he was instructed to press in the direction of the Confederate base of Brigadier General John Echols at the nearby town of Union. Colonel Augustus Moor would be sent south to Marling's Bottom by December 11 and push forward to threaten Lewisburg but remain in the vicinity of Frankford until December 18. General William Sullivan would be positioned in Woodstock within the Shenandoah Valley on December 11, and he would move to threaten Staunton on December 20 and 21. Colonel Joseph Thoburn would move on to the Parkersburg pike once he reached

Rhode Island's Ambrose Burnside had led brilliant amphibious attacks against North Carolina's Outer Banks early in the Civil War, commanded a corps at Antietam, and served briefly as commander of the Army of the Potomac at the disastrous battle at Fredericksburg, Virginia. Sent west to a new command, he was trapped in Knoxville as his men began to go hungry. The Confederates had broken their "cracker line."

Union General Benjamin F. Kelley had been involved in the war since its beginning. Wounded in the chest in the first land battle of the Civil War, Philippi, Kelley went on to become the commander of the entire region. His responsibilities included the defense of a crucial transportation route, the Baltimore and Ohio Railroad.

Monterey. His command would head for Staunton as well, in a feint to trick Confederate defenders into believing that Staunton was the object of the combined attack.

Averell's predeparture preparations were now complete. He had arranged for "demonstrations," or threatened attacks, against Confederate forces in Lewisburg from two possible directions, and two other forces were deployed into locations from which they could threaten Staunton. Averell hoped that Sullivan's movement toward Staunton and Scammon's threatened movement toward Union would provoke the defending Confederates into concentrating their forces, thus producing a wide gap in their lines through which his entire force could ship into the area, disrupt the railroad, and then ship back out without a fight.

All of the various units associated with Averell's plan began to move at one time. His mounted units left the post at New Creek near the Maryland border on December 8. Colonel Thoburn split from the main force on December 12 and moved according to plan. Obviously confused by the multiple movements of large Federal forces, the Confederate defenders began to react to these vaguely defined threats. Lewisburg and Union were obvious targets and it appeared that Staunton and its large store of supplies might be the intended point of these unusual midwinter moves.

Averell traveled over seldom-used back roads during a severe rainstorm that lasted two days, but the Union column made good progress and was able to penetrate deeply into Confederate territory without being detected. Travel was particulary difficult for the mounted men as most of the streams they had to cross did not have bridges. The majority of Averell's supply train, composed of wagons and ambulances, was sent along with Colonel Thoburn's infantry, and the sol-

Colonel Eliakim P. Scammon led a diversionary movement toward John Echols' base at Union, West Virginia, to add to the South's confusion about Averell's intended target. Soon, Scammon—promoted to general—fell victim to another raider, however, when Confederate Major Knowing snatched him from a riverboat anchored deep within Federal territory and delivered Scammon to Richmond. Soon, every mounted man in southern West Virginia was engaged in a search for Scammon.

diers were without the sparse comforts that they would have had.

Part of Averell's success to this point was due to the active patrolling that was done by his mounted scouts. Averell had been fortunate when he inherited a portion of Milroy's old command, including a scouting company that had been organized in St. Louis at the outbreak of the war. General John Frémont had ordered the formation of the scouts—who were expected to operate in the uniform of the enemy—at the urging of his wife, Jessie Benton Frémont. Once the scouts were organized, they were named "Jessie Scouts," in honor of the general's wife.

While many of these scouts, including their first commander, Charles Carpenter, were freebooters who were involved in the Federal war effort for what can be best described as "personal enrichment motives," several of the survivors had gained real military skills. Dressed in a Confederate uniform as often as they wore Federal blue, these scouts operated freely in a broad screen well to the front of Averell's primary column. Averell wrote in his report: "The head of my column was preceded by vigilant scouts, armed with repeating rifles, who permitted no one to go before them….My scouts thrown out kept me informed of the enemy's movements and positions."

Disguised in Confederate uniforms, the scouts were often able to approach and capture enemy couriers, and their dispatches were soon in Averell's hands. At least one message detailing troop movements, written by Major General Sam Jones, was captured and taken directly to Averell. Jones' dispatch had special instructions with the captured message: "The operator at Jackson's River will use every effort to get the above to General Early and a copy to Colonel Jackson. Colonel Jackson must have a copy of it."

Obviously, the message was not delivered to the local telegraph operator and both General Jubal Early and Colonel William Jackson were deprived of the advantageous early warning of Averell's movement. Without Jones' instructions, Confederate pursuit remained confused amid all the Federal maneuvering of troops.

It was thanks to his scouts that Averell was able to approach Salem, Virginia, and the target, the Virginia and Tennessee Railroad, before being detected. Four miles (6.5km) from Salem, a Confederate patrol met the lead elements of Averell's column. Without providing any details of the encounter, Averell reported that he learned from them that General Fitzhugh Lee had left

The Confederacy's John Echols maintained a significant force at his base near Union, West Virginia. Any movement by Averell would have to take Echols' presence into account, but the Federal plan actually took advantage of his presence by developing a feint toward him as Averell moved south toward the Virginia and Tennessee Railroad.

Lynchburg with the intention of intercepting the "Yankees" and that a train filled with troops was expected momentarily to guard the supplies accumulated at Salem for Longstreet's use in Tennessee. The Jessie Scouts had probably been able to intercept the Confederate patrol and engage them in conversation to gain this information. Based on this knowledge, a 350-man forward element rode into Salem on December 16 just before the arrival of the train filled the reinforcements from Lynchburg. Averell wrote in his report:

I hastened my advance, consisting of about 350 men and two three inch guns, through the town to the depot.

The telegraph wires were cut first—the operator was not to be found, the railroad track torn up in the vicinity of the depot, one gun placed in battery, and the advance dismounted and placed in readiness for the expected train of troops.

A train from Lynchburg, loaded with troops, soon approached. My main body was not yet in sight, and it was necessary to stop the train; a shot was fired at it from one of the guns, which missed; a second went through the train diagonally, which caused it to retire, and a third and last hastened its movements.

Averell was reinforced with the arrival of the rest of his column, and parties were sent along the tracks in both directions to destroy as much of the railroad as possible in the short time before additional Confederates arrived. Depots and their contents were burned and cars on the track, the "waterstation," the "turn-table," and five railroad bridges were destroyed by the raiders. Averell reported that private property was left untouched by his men and the citizens "received us with politeness."

After approximately six hours of destruction, the entire 4th Separate Brigade rode out of Salem to a position about seven miles (11km) from the town where they stopped to rest for the night. They had covered the last eighty miles (129km) to the doomed Confederate depot in an impressive thirty hours, and rest was needed by all. Averell's men planted misleading information by telling a few of the "polite" locals that they were planning to retreat from the area by way of the town of Buchanan, which was several miles to the east. The false information soon found its way to Fitzhugh Lee, who, believing it to be valid intelligence obtained through a lapse in security on the

part of some of the Union cavalrymen, led his men to the east and permitted Averell to escape from the noose that was being drawn tightly around him.

The Union commander was beginning to manage a near-miraculous escape from deep within a fully aroused and angry Confederate region. The earlier feints in the direction of Lewisburg and Staunton as well as a false advance by his men toward the town of Fincastle had confused the pursuit and spread the pursuers widely apart. Even so, the Jessie Scouts needed to secure the services of a local guide to take them through obscure country roads to safety.

Scouts rode into the small community of New Castle, Virginia, after discussing who in the region would be the best guide for the nearly trapped Union column. There were approximately twelve hundred Confederate troops in the vicinity under experienced commanders like Fitzhugh Lee, John Echols, John McCausland, and William L. "Mudwall" Jackson, so called to clearly distinguish him from his relative, "Stonewall."

Once the decision was made to impress a local guide, the scouts chose someone who would be in the best position to know all of the area's more obscure roads and trails: "Dr. Wylie," a man who would have ridden all of the back roads during the worst of weather. The country doctor was selected and advised that if he wanted to survive the war's current dangers, he would have to lead the entire command to the relative safety of West Virginia.

Leaving the campfires burning in the night, Averell was able to escape once more from the closely drawn Confederate traps that had been set for him. His corps reached the bridges over Jackson River near Covington and crossed at a gallop as the bridges had been filled with combustible materials and were set for destruction. One of Averell's regiments remained on the south

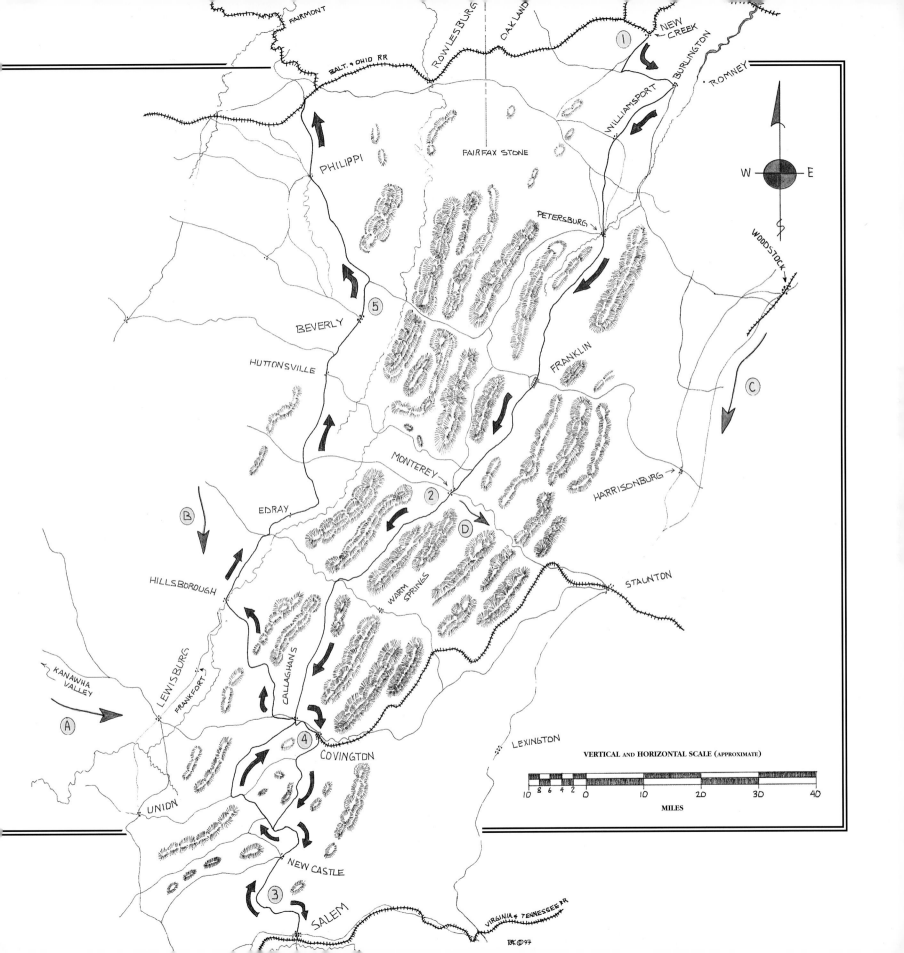

AVERELL'S DECEMBER RAID

side of the river to provide security as their wagons and ambulances crossed, but these were trapped when the Union commander ordered the bridges burned. Averell ordered the trapped regiment to swim their horses across the freezing, ice-filled river after destroying the wagons; four men drowned. A night attack against the regiment before the escape had cost the lives of five officers and 119 men.

Due to confused orders from General Kelley, the regiments that had been placed earlier into positions from which they would have been able to support Averell's retreat were no longer there. Nearly trapped, the Union column was nevertheless able to ride over obscure roads and trails to the Greenbrier River Valley, just inside the eastern boundary of West Virginia, as they continued north toward their base areas.

Averell's report illustrates best the conditions faced by his men:

On the way to Edray my rear guard experienced some trifling attacks on the 22nd. The road thence to Beverly was a glacier... traversed with great difficulty and peril. The artillery was drawn almost entirely by dismounted men during the 23rd and 24th. Couriers had been sent forward to Beverly to bring out subsistence and forage, which we succeeded, after extreme hardships, in meeting on the 24th.

The officers and men undertook all that was required of them, and endured all the sufferings from fatigue, hunger, and cold with extraordinary fortitude, even with cheerfulness. The march of 400 miles [644km], which was concluded at Beverly, was the most difficult I have ever seen performed.

The raid across the entire length of the new Union state, West Virginia, by twenty-five hundred Union soldiers had been more successful than anyone had ever hoped when the excursion into Confederate territory was ordered. Averell, through skillful planning and the careful deployment of his scouts, had managed to ride deeply into hostile territory for two weeks to destroy a major Confederate depot and disrupt a primary railroad communications route between Virginia and Tennessee. He lost relatively few men on the freezing trip, and his men were soon to receive the thanks of a grateful government. Secretary of War Edwin M. Stanton ordered that all the men on the raid be provided new suits, gratis, to replace those ruined by the rigors of the long trip.

With Averell's successful raid, the Union army had come a long way from James J. Andrews' failed raid on a similar railroad target early in the previous year.

Averell (second from left), and his officers developed an excellent plan of attack against a critical transportation route, the Virginia and Tennessee Railroad, which connected Virginia with the western theater of operation. Averell led bold cavalry raids against Confederate units and targets—at one stroke at Moorefield, West Virginia, be nearly eliminated Jubal Early's cavalry as an effective fighting force—but he was later relieved by Philip Sheridan, possibly to make room for a rival commander, Torbert. This photograph was taken during McClellan's Peninsula Campaign.

Grierson's Raid

An unlikely leader was finding his true vocation during the early part of the Civil War. Benjamin H. Grierson had been making his living as a musician and a music teacher when the war erupted; when he was assigned to the cavalry, he objected vigorously. He had been kicked by a pony as a child, hated horses, and desired nothing more than service far away from them. Nevertheless, the unlikely cavalry commander learned his trade as well as any-one else in the Union army, and he was soon recognized as a superb cavalry commander.

During the early spring of 1863, Ulysses S. Grant was in the process of developing his attacks against the Confederate strong point, Vicksburg, the last major obstacle preventing the Union from grasping total control of the length of the Mississippi River. Union control of the river would effectively split the Confederacy into two isolated sections. Defending against this major campaign was the Confederacy's General John Pemberton and a force that out-numbered Grant's attackers. The plan was audacious and Grant was faced with the loss of his entire army if he failed.

Pemberton was responsible for the defense of a broad area and Grant took advantage of

Benjamin Grierson was an unlikely cavalry commander. A music teacher who hated horses, this Federal officer was soon to lead effective, well-planned raids into the Confederacy. During Grant's Vicksburg campaign, Grierson led a raid that crossed the entire breadth of the Confederacy as large Rebel units searched for him in all directions. His masterly use of deception prevented his apprehension and the destruction of his command.

this by sending out large forces to keep his Confederate opponent confused as to the true intentions of the Union army. Division-sized elements of Grant's army were dispatched to the north and northwest of Vicksburg, but Grant's most daring diversionary move would be a cavalry raid from La Grange, Tennessee, across Mississippi to link up with Federal forces in the vicinity of Baton Rouge, Louisiana. The commander chosen for the dangerous operation was Benjamin Grierson.

Grierson's orders were given as broadly as possible to allow him to modify his plan as needed as the military situation facing him changed. With the Union army positioned in west Tennessee and northern Louisiana, Grierson's raiding party would be able to disrupt the Confederate lines of communication—actually cutting the Confederacy temporarily in half—while leaving the Confederate army under Pemberton confused as to his intentions. Pemberton's staff planners would anticipate a deep strike into their territory before the raiding party would ride swiftly back into Tennessee. The Union plan assumed that Confederate forces would react to Grierson's presence by concentrating along his probable line of withdrawal rather than by attempting to cut

him off from his true destination, a link-up with Federal forces far to his south. The plan was good and the commander was brave and capable of completing it.

He was ordered to ride from La Grange, Tennessee, in a general southerly direction through Mississippi along a route that would allow him to strike at the region's two north-south railroads and permit the destruction of the major east-west railroad that connected Vicksburg with the eastern part of the Confederacy. The tactical goals of the raiding force included the burning of military supplies found along the route while they provoked reactions from local Confederate commanders—preventing them from concentrating against Grant.

Grierson and his seventeen hundred cavalrymen left their camps at La Grange on April 17 and moved south. They quickly encountered small groups of Confederate militia and regular soldiers who were easily brushed aside by the large Federal cavalry force. On the fourth day, Grierson used an excellent deception maneuver to throw his pursuers off of his trail. He sent a report back to his headquarters that outlined his intentions:

At 3 o'clock the next morning, April 20, I

detached 175 of the least effective portion of the command, with one gun of the battery and all the prisoners, led horses, and captured property, under the command of Major Love, of the Second Iowa, to proceed back to La Grange, marching in columns of four, before daylight, through Pontotoc, and thus leaving the impression that the whole command had returned.

Grierson had decided to confuse his pursuers. His "less effective portion of the command" included his sick and injured men who would slow his march as they moved south. These men, called the "Quinine Brigade" by the remaining cavalrymen, returned to Tennessee in a column that rode four abreast to make their numbers appear larger than they actually were. The sick men were sent on the route that the Confederates assumed Grierson would be taking as he returned to the safety of La Grange and they quickly set off in pursuit— giving Grierson an additional ten hours' head start.

The following day, April 21, Grierson repeated his successful deception by sending another large group, an entire cavalry regiment—the 2nd Iowa Cavalry—off to the east toward

a Confederate base area before turning north to safety and Tennessee. Grierson reported:

The following morning at 6 o'clock I resumed the march southward, and about 8 o'clock came to the road leading southeast to Columbus, Miss. Here I detached Colonel Hatch, with the Second Iowa Cavalry and one gun of the battery, with orders to proceed to the Mobile and Ohio Railroad in the vicinity of West Point, and destroy the road and wires; thence move south, destroying the railroad and all public property as far south, if possible, as Macon; thence across the railroad, making a circuit northward; if practicable, take Columbus and destroy all Government works in that place, and again strike the railroad south of Okolona, and, destroying it, return to La Grange by the most practicable route.

Colonel Hatch and his 2nd Iowa Cavalry had to make a fast march of 175 miles (282km) before they reached La Grange, but Grierson's ruse worked flawlessly. Hatch was pursued closely by the only major Confederate force in the area and Grierson continued to move south as his Confederate pursuers marched north after Hatch and his Iowa cavalrymen, believing that this was the entire Federal raiding force. Hatch actually outnumbered those in pursuit and could have defeated them in open battle, but he merely engaged in a fighting withdrawal in order to continue the illusion that the entire force was returning to La Grange.

Remaining unchallenged, Grierson continued on his march deep into Southern territory. He had developed a very effective scouting capability and his scouts, dressed in Confederate uniform and subject to execution as spies if captured, moved freely to Grierson's front and flanks as they rode swiftly to capture strategic points prior to the arrival of the Federal main body. They captured bridges before they could be destroyed and scouted for the presence of the enemy before Grierson could be attacked by larger forces that could possibly eliminate his raiders.

Colonel Grierson was actively sending out small parties in several directions to deceive the Confederates as to his real intentions. On April 22, he sent thirty-five men of the 7th Illinois Cavalry to the east toward the town of Macon to destroy telegraph lines there.

He made careful use of all of the assets at his disposal, occasionally relying on single brave scouts:

I sent a single scout, disguised as a citizen, to proceed northward to the line of the Southern Railroad, cut the telegraph, and, if possible, fire a bridge or trestle-work. He started on his journey about midnight, and when within 7 miles [11km] of the railroad he came upon a regiment of Southern cavalry from Brandon, Miss., in search of us. He succeeded in misdirecting them as to the place where he had last seen us, and, having seen them well on the wrong road, he immediately retraced his steps to camp with the news. When he first met them they were on the direct road to our camp, and had they not been turned from their course would have come up with us before daylight.

Grierson had been saved by the actions of a single brave man who would have been hanged had it been discovered that he was a Union soldier in civilian clothing. The oncoming Confederates would have caught Grierson's command

"before daylight" in their night camps and would have decimated the Union soldiers.

The remainder of Grierson's "Butternut Guerrillas" moved in advance of the regular troops and entered the town of Newton Station on April 24. Disguised as Confederates, they were able to learn that there were two trains due to arrive at the strategic town and one of them, a freight train bound for Vicksburg and loaded with supplies for the garrison there, was captured as it pulled on to a siding. Grierson soon ordered his men to burn all of the military supplies, and destroy as much track as possible. Grierson further ordered that two captured locomotives be blown up. The commander described the scene in his report:

Lieutenant-Colonel Blackburn dashed into the town, took possession of the railroad and telegraph, and succeeded in capturing two trains in less than half an hour after his arrival. One of these, 25 cars, was loaded with ties and machinery, and the other 13 cars were loaded with commissary stores and ammunition, among the latter several thousand loaded shells. These, together with a large

quantity of commissary and quartermaster's stores and about five hundred stand of arms stored in the town, were destroyed. Seventy-five prisoners captured at this point were paroled. The locomotives were exploded and otherwise rendered completely unserviceable. Here the track was torn up, and a bridge half a mile west of the station destroyed.

By early afternoon, his command was back in the saddle and moving west.

It was at this time that Confederate General Pemberton began to take Grierson seriously and he sent units throughout the region to trap him—just as Grant had hoped when the raid was ordered. The overall tactical picture, however, was muddied by the presence and actions taken by the independent commands sent out from Grierson's column. Colonel Hatch was still moving back toward La Grange, Tennessee, and the thirty-five men of the 7th Illinois Cavalry were still in the vicinity of Macon and confused the situation for the Confederates.

Grierson and the main column continued to move westward as Colonel Hatch retreated slowly back to Tennessee and the men of the 7th Illinois attempted to locate and rejoin the main force. By April 27, the small detachment had found Grierson, and Hatch had reached safety in Tennessee, but the Union commander knew that time was running out for his command. They were deep within enemy territory, exhausted from riding thirty-five miles (56km) each day, and living off the land. They were within fifty miles of their planned destination, Grand Gulf, a town on the Mississippi River that Grant had planned to use for an amphibious landing, but there were no indications that the landing had actually happened. There were no rumors, refugees, or prisoner reports of any Federal landing in the vicinity, and Grierson was concerned that he could lose his entire force by capture. He wrote in his report:

Hearing nothing more of our forces at Grand Gulf, I concluded to make for Baton Rouge to recruit my command, after which I could return to La Grange, through Southern Mississippi and Western Alabama; or, crossing the Mississippi River, move through Louisiana and Arkansas.

He had taken the decision to make his escape, but the safety of Baton Rouge was still 150 miles (241km) away. His worn-

Kicked by a pony as a child, Benjamin Grierson feared horses as much as he disliked them. Fate, however, had placed him in the Federal cavalry, and Grierson soon developed himself into a dashing, able cavalry commander in the western theater of operations. His raid across Mississippi left General Pemberton, the Confederate commander at Vicksburg, confused about Grant's intentions until it was too late for Pemberton to concentrate Confederate forces against him.

out men and their horses were suffering from the extended march they had been forced to make, although they replaced their mounts from local sources whenever they had an opportunity. But they had managed to avoid any direct combat with the Confederate forces that were spreading throughout the region to trap them. After two full weeks in the saddle, Grierson ran into trouble on May 1 at a bridge guarded by Louisiana Partisan Rangers and suffered five men wounded and an additional five men captured. Grierson was forced to leave his wounded men behind at a local plantation as he continued the retreat. Confederate forces in large numbers were swarming in the area and he and his exhausted regiments had to continue riding if they were to reach safety. They rode all night, many of the men so exhausted that they had to tie themselves to their saddles to remain mounted, but they arrived within four miles (6.5km) of the Union lines at Baton Rouge the following day, where the men were allowed to stop for rest. They had successfully pulled off a daring and ambitious raid across the width of the Confederacy.

Grierson described the results of his raid:

These two historic photographs were taken by a Confederate secret agent, Lytle, within minutes of one another. They show Grierson's command safely arrived at Baton Rouge, Louisiana, after an epic raid that covered 600 miles (965 km) through hostile territory over a period of sixteen days. The photograph on the left was taken first; the photograph on the right shows a covered wagon that has just arrived on the scene.

During the expedition we killed and wounded about 100 of the enemy, captured and paroled over 500 prisoners, many of them officers, destroyed between 50 [80km] and 60 miles [97km] of railroad and telegraph, captured and destroyed over 3,000 stand of arms, and other army stores and Government property to an immense amount; we also captured 1,000 horses and mules.

Our loss during the entire journey was 3 killed, 7 wounded, 5 left on the route sick; the sergeant-major and surgeon of the Seventh Illinois left with Lieutenant-Colonel Blackburn, and 9 men missing, supposed to have straggled. We marched over 600 miles [965km] in less than sixteen days. The last twenty-eight hours we marched 76 miles [122km], had four engagements with the enemy, and forded the Comite River, which was deep enough to swim many of the horses. During this time the men and horses were without food or rest.

chapter 4

A GRAY GHOST CAPTURES A GENERAL

The Confederacy was blessed with men who had practically grown up in the saddle. For this reason, the South's cavalry was able to dominate its Federal counterpart during the first half of the Civil War. There were, however, many men who for a variety of reasons did not adjust well to the discipline and regimentation of the regular army. These rugged individualists were more than willing to ride deeply into Federal country at the head of a Partisan Ranger band and do battle behind their opponent's lines.

One of these men was John Singleton Mosby, a 125-pound (57kg) twenty-seven-year-old with a bad temper and a poor attitude toward his West Point commander, Fitzhugh Lee. Mosby had done well in the cavalry, rising from private to lieutenant in a short time, but the discipline of the regular

officers was too much for him. After he had incurred the wrath of Fitzhugh Lee for calling a bugle a horn, Mosby realized that his career opportunities within the First Virginia Cavalry could be limited. He resigned his commission, as officers were permitted to do, and volunteered to serve as a scout for Jeb Stuart, the officer who had assisted Robert E. Lee with the resolution of John Brown's attack on Harpers Ferry.

As a scout, captured then released shortly after, Mosby demonstrated to his superior officers that he was quite capable of collecting intelligence on enemy activities. This ability, combined with his desire for independent duty far from senior officers, convinced Stuart that Mosby and nine men should be left in northern Virginia to begin operations as a Partisan Ranger in December 1862.

"In one sense the charge that I did not fight fair is true. I fought for success and not for display. There was no man in the Confederate army who had less of the spirit of knight-errantry in him, or who took a more practical view of war than I did."

—John Singleton Mosby

PAGE 51: *John Singleton Mosby, photographed in 1863 at the height of his activities against the Union army, bears himself with the confidence of a soldier at the peak of his skills. He was the commander of a battalion of accomplished Confederate cavalrymen who had carried the war into the previously secure rear areas of the Union forces, in the immediate vicinity of Washington, D.C. Early in Mosby's guerrilla career, he planned a raid with the goal of capturing a British officer, Percy Wyndham (left), who had belittled him publicly. Wyndham was absent, but with the assistance of a Union army deserter, Mosby was able to capture Brigadier General Edwin H. Stoughton, the youngest general in the Union army. It was Mosby's inability to adapt to the military discipline demanded by West Point graduate Fitzhugh Lee (above) that led the future raider to independent service. Lee, demanding strict adherence to all traditions and customs of military life, became angry when he heard Mosby call a bugle a "horn."*

John Mosby and a few of the men who served with him in the 43rd Battalion of Partisan Rangers. Most of his men lived in Loudoun County, Virginia, the area where the majority of their operations were conducted, and they all received support and intelligence on enemy activities from a network of friends and relatives spread throughout the region.

Mosby's achievements were such that by the middle of January, he was attracting unwanted attention from Union commanders in the area. His swift, silent raids on isolated sentry positions had netted twenty-two prisoners in a very short period. In response to this new challenge, Colonel Percy Wyndham, an experienced British soldier of fortune, began sending large forces into the area in an effort to locate and eliminate the disruptive guerrilla force.

"No human being knows how sweet sleep is but a soldier."

—*John Singleton Mosby*

An odd feud between the partisan leader and the former soldier of fortune began when the frustrated Union colonel was told by paroled prisoners that the man who had captured them had sent a verbal message. The Union horsemen were advised that if they weren't better armed and equipped, it wouldn't pay to capture them.

Mosby had been scouting the region around the Federal camps near Fairfax, Virginia, for some time. In his efforts, he was

John Singleton Mosby enjoyed posing for photographs during the war. This was taken in Richmond in January 1863, and a note on a print written later by Mosby states, "The uniform is the one I wore on March 8th, 1863 on the night of General Stoughton's capture."

each rider was armed with a saber and two pistols when captured.

The personal feud between these two enemies became more personal as Mosby's raids continued and Wyndham found that he was unable to halt them. In early March, Mosby captured another nineteen officers and men near Middleburg, and the newspapers let out a howl of protest over the poor management of the cavalry that permitted these disasters to continue.

Mosby, aided by a recent deserter from the 1st New York Cavalry—"Big Yank" Ames, who had deserted from his regiment over the Emancipation Proclamation—approached the sleeping village where Percy Wyndham was living. Mosby and twenty-nine of his men decided to make a night call on the outspoken Englishman who had challenged them from a distance.

Nearby, there was a house where the commander of the 2nd Vermont Brigade, Edwin H. Stoughton, slept after a late party. Stoughton had recently become the youngest general officer in Federal service at the age of twenty-four; the Vermont native, a member of a wealthy family, was a West Point graduate. Unfortunately, he enjoyed entertaining the ladies—one twenty-year-old woman had been quartered in a well-guarded tent located near Stoughton's headquarters—and this night had been special. His mother and sister were visiting from Vermont and had attended an evening champagne party planned for the occasion. All of Stoughton's officers had been there and the pleasant night had been enjoyed by all.

Colonel Wyndham, the recipient of only bad luck since Mosby had been left in his area of responsibility by Stuart the previous December, was finally to be lucky. He had been summoned unexpectedly to Washington and, with regrets, missed Stoughton's party.

Late in the night, as the last of the revelers had departed to their homes and quarters, riders approached the single sentry who was slowly patrolling in the small town. With the enemy at least twenty-five miles (40km)

aided by a young woman, Antonia Ford, the daughter of a local merchant whose brother was serving in the artillery. Mosby disguised himself as a citizen and remained in the Ford home for three nights as they collected information on the enemy.

After reporting to Stuart that the Federal cavalry was isolated from the rest of the Union army at Fairfax and vulnerable to attack, Stuart urged that an attempt be made to capture Wyndham. Late in February, Mosby, with twenty-six men, was able to capture an outpost of forty Union cavalrymen and their horses, an act that infuriated the already frustrated Wyndham. He continued the verbal feud with the partisan leader by publicly denouncing him as an ordinary horse thief. Mosby responded to the charge by dryly noting that all of the horses he had stolen had riders to go with them, and that

Mosby and his men seemed to be everywhere and the large section of northern Virginia where they operated most frequently became known—especially among Union soldiers—as Mosby's Confederacy.

Mosby and his men became a painful thorn in the side of the Union army in northen Virginia. Long rides, sudden attacks, and swift withdrawals became the hallmarks of these Confederate Partisan Rangers as they sabotaged the Union army's lines of communication.

A Gray Ghost Captures a General

A Gray Ghost Captures a General

Gordon Phillips ©

ABOVE: Fairfax Court House, Virginia, photographed in June 1863. It was in this small town that General Stoughton had decided to host a champagne party—at the time of Mosby's arrival, Stoughton was sleeping off the effects of his party in a bedroom. LEFT: Mosby and his raiders struck swiftly, without warning, and frequently escaped without losses. Lonely outposts were normally their targets, but they often raided against Federal supply lines. Careful scouting operations ensured successful attacks.

away and roads that were bottomless mud holes, the picket didn't bother to sound an alarm. These lonely riders had to be returning Union cavalrymen. Slowly, they split into smaller groups; one went to the telegrapher's tent while another rode directly to the lonely picket, surprising him by brandishing pistols directly in his face. One group rode to the house where their English quarry was reported to be sleeping.

Stoughton's aide opened the door of his residence when the men outside announced that dispatches had arrived for the general. He was more than mildly surprised when a short man with a plume in his hat shoved a pistol into his chest and hushed him. Immediately afterward, John Mosby was inside Stoughton's bedroom, where he raised the nightshirt of the sleeping general and whacked him across the rear to awaken him.

More than a little confused, Stoughton asked Mosby if Fitzhugh Lee was present. Lying behind a smile, Mosby said that his former senior officer was there. Stoughton asked to be taken to him as "I knew him at West Point."

Mosby had missed his intended target, Colonel Wyndham, but he had captured a brigadier general instead. The total yield from Fairfax Court House was larger than anticipated: the raiders left with a brigadier general, two captains, thirty privates, and fifty-eight horses.

When advised of the results of the raid, President Lincoln came out with one of his more memorable statements on the war:

"Well, I'm sorry for that. I can make new brigadier generals, but I can't make horses."

Antonia Ford, Mosby's co-conspirator within the Union camp, was soon arrested for her complicity in the raid, and she spent months in a Federal prison. Subsisting on a diet of rice and poor-quality meat, she was pale and thin by the time she was sent through the lines to Richmond. A year and a day after the successful raid, she married Major Joseph Willard, a Union officer who had been quartered in her home early in the war, but she was dead within seven years, possibly a victim of the poor diet she had lived on while in prison.

Mosby continued his active military career for the remainder of the Civil War. By late spring, he had attacked a train delivering supplies for Joseph Hooker's army that was located to the north of the Rappahannock River, and fought a major battle with an overwhelming force of Union cavalry. The partisans escaped after fierce hand-to-hand combat with their pursuers and enjoyed the supplies looted from the train. The men had done such a good job fighting behind the enemy's lines that the Confederate War Department officially designated them the "43rd Battalion of Virginia Cavalry" on June 10, 1863.

The men of the 43rd Battalion continued their fight against the Union army, striking where they were least expected. They were in near-constant motion and their success was noticed by both General Lee and the Confederate War Department. Lee wrote that in the previous six months Mosby had killed, wounded, or captured twelve hundred Federals and had taken more than sixteen hundred horses and mules, 230 head of cattle, and eighty-five wagons and ambulances.

Mosby and his men continued to conduct successful operations even as the Confederate Congress ordered all of the Partisan Ranger companies disbanded. They

had become havens for able-bodied men seeking to avoid the draft, and as often as not, they would rob Confederate citizens as readily as they would Union sympathizers. Only the 43rd Battalion of John Mosby and the men serving to the west under Hanse McNeil were exempt from the order to disband.

Some of Mosby's major operations included attacks against the Federal crews seeking to repair the Manassas Gap Railroad, a supply line that, when opened, would have permitted General Sheridan to move south toward the vital railroads that passed through Charlottesville. In early October 1864, guerrilla raids resulted in derailed and wrecked trains and captured Union guards. Repairs to the line were never completed. By the middle of October, the raiders had set an ambush for another train, this time on the vulnerable B&O. After loosening a rail from its cross ties, the men settled down to rest, but were roused by a loud explosion from a rupturing steam-engine boiler. They captured an army payroll that was on the train, and Mosby's men rode from the scene with $170,000 in Federal greenbacks.

"It is just as legitimate to fight an enemy in the rear as in the front. The only difference is in the danger."

—John Singleton Mosby

Speedy riders and good intelligence collected from supporters and family members living within their area of operations enabled Mosby's men to engage in sudden attacks that were especially dreaded by Union soldiers. They knew Mosby seldom struck without a high probability of success.

Mosby nearly died of wounds that he sustained when a Union cavalry patrol fired at him through a window in a house where he had stopped to have a late dinner with friends one December evening. Quickly removing his officer's insignia, he lay on the floor—bleeding from what should have been fatal injuries—and gave a false name to the officer who came to interrogate him. Left to die, Mosby nevertheless recovered and continued his activities for the remainder of the Civil War.

He disbanded his men at Salem and they went their different ways. The battalion had suffered severe casualties. Somewhere between 35 to 40 percent of the command was killed, wounded, or captured during the war. Eighty-five of the men were either killed or mortally wounded, or were executed when captured by their enemies. More than one hundred men were wounded in combat and another 477 were captured.

After the war, Mosby was denied the opportunity to surrender, and lived as a fugitive. He evaded capture for nearly two months by hiding near the homes of family members until he was paroled through the direct intervention of Grant at the end of June 1865. He resumed his law practice at home with his family. He became friends with Grant, became a Republican and was condemned in the South for it, and was appointed to positions in the Federal government, including consul in Hong Kong for eight years. At the age of eighty-two in 1916, John Mosby died after a long, adventuresome life.

Confederate veterans, survivors of Mosby's 43rd Battalion of Partisan Rangers, were proud of their hazardous service and they met at reunions with family members.

"To destroy supply trains, to break up the means of conveying intelligence, and thus isolating an army from its base, as well as its different corps from each other, to confuse their plans by capturing despatches, are the objects of partisan war."

—John Singleton Mosby, 1887

Mosby survived the dangers of war, but he was initally refused the opportunity to surrender after Appomattox. General Grant intervened and Mosby was able to return to his law practice in Virginia. Mosby never forgot Grant's gallant act; he later became a Republican and served as U.S. consul in Hong Kong.

A GRAY GHOST CAPTURES A GENERAL

chapter 5

JONES' AND IMBODEN'S THIRTY DAY RAIDS

Large numbers of Union soldiers were about to lose a great deal of sleep as the spring campaign of 1863 opened in the mountainous region of what was then northwestern Virginia, and today is part of West Virginia. This region of Virginia had fallen under the control of the Union army after the bumbling campaigns led by former Virginia governors Henry A. Wise and John B. Floyd in late 1861. Their personal feuding combined with their lack of military ability had resulted in a general evacuation from the strategic, resource-filled Kanawha Valley. Confederate General W.W. Loring's invasion of the region in September 1862 also failed when the fractious officer chose to ignore—or misunderstood—his orders, and after great initial successes his small army was forced to retreat from the area.

Local Unionists, backed by strong contingents of Federal soldiers, were encouraged sufficiently by Confederate failures in the region to form a "loyal" government as well as a "New State Movement." With a new government in the northern city of Wheeling, the Union supporters were close to the formation of their new state, West Virginia, which would be a major political victory for the hard-pressed federal government in Washington, D.C. The splitting of a major Confederate state, Virginia, would represent a political and moral victory for the national government at a time when it was sorely needed.

The success of a raid into Federally controlled western Virginia would have several benefits for the Confederacy. First, the New State Movement would be shaken to its core

PAGE 63: John D. Imboden began the Civil War as an artillery officer and fought gallantly at Henry House Hill during the Battle of Bull Run. Soon, he was organizing the 1st Virginia Partisan Rangers, and commanding a full cavalry brigade. After the raid into western Virginia, he participated in Lee's Gettysburg Campaign by raiding along the Baltimore and Ohio Railroad, assisting with wagon-train escort duties, and fighting as part of the rear guard as the Confederate army withdrew from Pennsylvania. ABOVE: General William W. Loring had served in the Mexican War as a major, a conflict in which Robert E. Lee served as a captain. Loring's loss of an arm and his reputation as a warrior produced unrealistic expectations of success when he took the field. He led a successful invasion of the strategic Kanawha Valley in western Virginia during the summer of 1862, but he failed to hold the area for the Confederacy.

as the raiders moved at will through its territory—a demonstration of a capability that could be repeated at any time in the future. A new Federal state would not necessarily become a safe area for Unionists, and the raiders planned to show their Unionist enemies that there would be a price for their betrayal of Virginia. Second, the attackers intended to destroy as much of the property of the Baltimore and Ohio Railroad as was possible. The strategic rail system was the southernmost line of supply that linked the western Union states with the battlefields in the eastern theater, and its destruction would delay the arrival of supplies and reinforcements that would be detoured over railroads further to the north. Finally, the region to be invaded was a rich source of horses, cattle, general supplies, and, most important, new recruits who could be added to the rolls of the Confederate army.

Two experienced officers—William E. Jones, who was known as "Grumble" to his men, and John D. Imboden—would lead the two small armies that would operate independently for most of the incursion. From the time they left their camps, which were located just to the east of the mountainous region, on April 20, 1863, until they returned on May 22, their Union opponents would have little opportunity to catch up on the sleep they were missing. The Union force garrisoning western Virginia was spread thinly in several isolated outposts, and reinforcements were slow to be ordered to march to the assistance of threatened points. A general panic had seized the Union commanders as Jones and Imboden began their independent marches. Swift movement—even by the largely infantry and dismounted cavalry forces of the Confederates—confused the Federal commanders, and each key point felt threatened. The overall commander in the area, Brigadier General Benjamin S. Roberts, was unable to order his scattered men to

concentrate at a single location to face the raiders in a decisive battle. Each small, isolated detachment of Union soldiers had to face the raiders alone, and the raiders appeared to be everywhere simultaneously.

Imboden was the first to move. He marched his invading force out of his camp on Shenandoah Mountain on April 20, the day before Jones' planned departure. This force, made up chiefly of infantrymen, would naturally be expected to move slower. It was composed of the 22nd, 25th, 31st, and 62nd Virginia infantries, the 18th and 19th regiments, the 37th Battalion, some Virginia Cavalry, and McClanahan's Battery. The total force was 3,365 men and six guns, but only seven hundred of the cavalrymen were mounted. The remainder were expected to obtain mounts during the raid by either capture or purchase.

The first four days of the long march were among the worst as the tired men struggled forward along the Parkersburg pike's and Staunton Turnpike's soaked roads during drenching rainstorms. They arrived at Huttonsville in the Tygarts Valley after the first seventy miles (113km), where within only a few miles the first major Federal garrison, at Beverly—the 2nd West Virginia Infantry Regiment and a few soldiers from the 8th West Virginia, in all about nine hundred men—waited in complete ignorance of the Confederate army that was advancing against them.

Imboden ordered an attack on April 24. The surprised Federal soldiers put up a stiff resistance. They were able to hold out until late in the evening, when their commander, Colonel Latham of the 2nd West Virginia, ordered a retreat toward Philippi, the location of the first land battle of the war, after ordering that fire be set to all government supplies that could not be easily moved. Part of the town was unfortunately burned as well, but Latham's men escaped. Imboden ordered a cavalry pursuit, and the retreating Federal soldiers were chased for only a short distance. There were few casualties in this first skirmish of the extended incursion: no one was killed and only a few men received wounds.

"Grumble" Jones ordered his small army from its camp at Lacey Springs, Virginia, on April 21. His force was composed of the 7th, 11th, and 12th Virginia Cavalry regiments and White's, Brown's, and Witcher's cavalry battalions. Jones had a few small infantry units and artillery attached to his force. They arrived at Moorefield in West Virginia's Hardy County and found that the south branch of the Potomac River was so swollen by the recent spring rains that they could not cross. After ordering his infantry and artillery support back to their base areas in the Shenandoah Valley, Jones led his column south to Petersburg, where they were able to cross the dangerous river.

The following day, Jones took a side road that would take his men to the Northwestern Turnpike, where they could travel quickly to their selected targets. Once they entered Greenland Gap, a force of eighty men from the 23rd Illinois and the 14th West Virginia Infantry regiments disputed their passage. The greatly outnumbered Union soldiers took cover in a log church and house, and a brisk but hopeless fight ensued. In a short time, the defenders were forced to surrender after two of their men were killed and several wounded. Jones had lost four men; ten were wounded.

When the Confederate raiders began to be reported over a broad region in western Virginia, the Union's commander in the region, General Benjamin Roberts, was unable to concentrate his widely dispersed men at a single point to face them. Unable to react, Roberts and his men were forced to remain in place to face Jones' or Imboden's attacks alone.

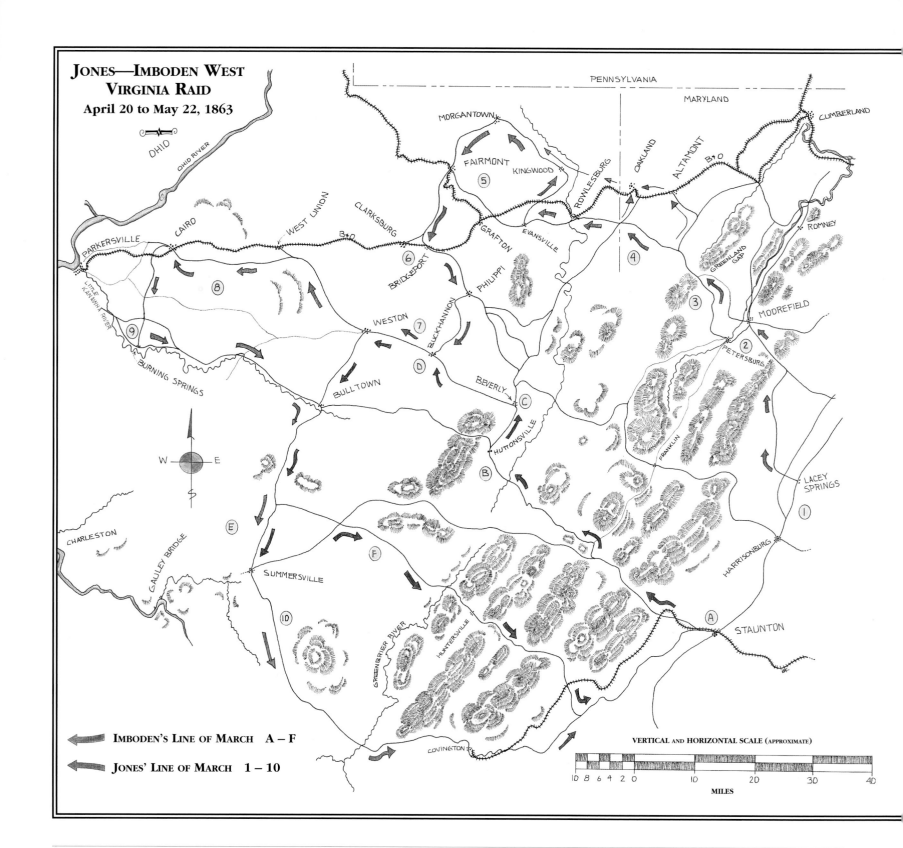

JONES—IMBODEN WEST VIRGINIA RAID
April 20 to May 22, 1863

IMBODEN'S LINE OF MARCH   A – F

JONES' LINE OF MARCH   1 – 10

VERTICAL AND HORIZONTAL SCALE (APPROXIMATE)

10 8 6 4 2 0   10   20   30   40

MILES

JONES' AND IMBODEN'S THIRTY DAY RAIDS

A. Imboden departed Staunton on April 20 en route to Beverly.

1. Jones departed Lacey Springs on April 21.

B. On April 23 Imboden's forces reached Huttonsville

2. Jones reached Moorefield on April 23. High water on the South Branch of the Potomac forced Jones to leave behind his infantry and artillery.

C. After a two-hour struggle Imboden captured Beverly on April 24.

3. On April 25 Union forces delayed Jones for over four hours at Greenland Gap.

4. Jones split his force into three sections. The main section went to Rowlesburg and two smaller sections went to Oakland and Altamont. On April 26 Jones failed to capture Rowlesburg and marched through Evansville and Kingwood to Morgantown. On April 28 the Oakland and Altamont groups rejoined Jones near Fairmont.

D. On April 28 Imboden occupied Buckhannon and waited for Jones.

5. On April 29 Jones attacked Union forces at Fairmont and destroyed the suspension bridge over the Monongahela.

6. On April 30 Jones captured a company of Federal soldiers at Bridgeport. May 1 he passed through Philippi.

7. On May 2 Jones rejoined Imboden at Buckhannon. Both then moved to Weston. On May 6 Jones headed northwest toward Parkersville.

E. Imboden went south to Summersville, captured a Union wagon train, and waited for Jones.

8. Part of Jones' force attacked West Union while the other damaged a rail tunnel and burned bridges at Cairo.

9. On May 9, Jones burned the oil fields at Burning Springs along the Little Kanawha River.

10. Jones rejoined Imboden on April 14 at Summersville. Both agreed little more could be accomplished and returned to the Shenandoah via seperate routes; Jones through Lewisburg and Covington.

F. Imboden returned through Huntersville.

Very real danger lay in wait for the solitary courier. Raiders would often ambush or sweep up as captives unfortunate soldiers assigned to this perilous and unpleasant duty.

As they ascended into the high, freezing mountain, Jones began to send selected detachments to destroy their targets. Colonel Harman's group, composed of the 12th Virginia Cavalry, Brown's Maryland Battalion, and McNeil's Rangers, were sent to cut the telegraph wires and destroy the railroad bridges at Oakland before marching west to rejoin the main column at Morgantown. Others were sent to burn railroad bridges twelve miles (19km) east of Oakland. The widely spread detachments made Jones' column appear larger than it actually was and panic spread throughout the region.

Harman rode along the Pennsylvania border, spreading panic as he went, and he entered Morgantown during the afternoon of April 27. After a short occupation of the town, they left and rejoined Jones, but the entire force returned to Morgantown again at noon on April 28. Many of the men who had fled the town with their horses returned only to lose their mounts to the invaders. The men were on their best behavior and guards were posted at local saloons to ensure that they remained sober. They left Morgantown after dark and rode south to Fairmont.

Gaining the opposite side of the town before the Federal garrison could retreat, the Southern cavalry was soon charging through the streets. The few soldiers assigned there, 260 of them, were soon secured as prisoners and the town was occupied. A train loaded with troops and artillery arrived from nearby Grafton, but these were held at bay while Jones' engineers prepared to destroy a very expensive target: the iron bridge over the Monongahela River.

This structure, the most expensive bridge on the entire railroad (it cost nearly half a million dollars to build), was 615 feet (187.5m) long and supported by tubular columns of cast iron resting on stone piers in the river. The engineers poured black powder into the hollow tubular structures and ignited fuses, but the large explosions did no damage to the large bridge. Jones ordered that the wooden parts of the bridge be burned. After this was done, a final attempt with black powder was tried, and by nightfall the last spans of the expensive structure lay in the water.

At this time, Jones headed east and marched directly at the large Union stronghold at Clarksburg, and turned only when his lead elements had struck the outer defenses. They struck hard at the railroad in the small town of Bridgeport, six miles (9.5km) from Clarksburg, and destroyed a train and all of the bridges and trestles they could locate nearby. Once this was accomplished Jones ordered a march toward Buckhannon, where he hoped to unite his force with that of Imboden.

Imboden had roamed through the region slowly, scouring the territory for supplies and horses for his command to take back to Virginia. He entered Buckhannon on April 29 while Jones was busily blasting away at the long bridge at Fairmont, and he waited for Jones' arrival. After a short period of rest, the commanders decided to call off their planned attack against Clarksburg, as the garrison had been reinforced, and Imboden was sent south toward Summersville with the wagon trains and captured livestock. Jones would continue operations against the railroad while attracting attention to his cavalrymen as Imboden's infantry marched slowly in the direction of safety.

Harman and his large detached force destroyed two bridges in the vicinity of West Union and captured ninety soldiers in the

While en route to a new assignment before the war, Confederate William E. Jones lost his wife when a huge wave swept her overboard. The loss deeply affected Jones, who was easily angered and became known as "Grumble" to his men. He served the Confederacy well until his own death during the Battle of Piedmont in 1864.

process of occupying the town. Jones moved farther toward the end of the B&O, to the Ohio River city of Parkersburg, but after receiving reports that the city had been reinforced by Ohio troops, he drew back from the planned attack there. In the vicinity of the small town of Cairo, his men leisurely burned three additional railroad bridges and destroyed a tunnel by filling it with cribbed wood and setting the wood on fire. The heat of the intense fires damaged the tunnel's roof and it caved in, blocking it from future train use for some time.

Immediately afterward, Jones marched his small army to Oiltown, the location of the Burning Springs oil field and the drilling operations there. On May 9, his soldiers completely smashed the field's drilling equip-

ment and set fire to the stored oil, destroying an oil refinery operation for the first time in warfare. Jones was elated with the damage he had created and wrote in his report:

All the oil, the tanks, barrels, engines for pumping, engine houses and wagons—in a word everything used for raising, holding, or sending it off was burned. The smoke is very dense and jet black. The boats, filled with oil in bulk, burst with a report almost equaling artillery, and spread the burning fluid over the river. Before night huge columns of ebon smoke marked the meanderings of the stream as far as the eye could reach. By dark the oil from the tanks on the burning creek had reached the river, and the whole stream became a sheet of fire. A burning river, carrying destruction to our merciless enemy, was a scene of magnificence that might well carry joy to every patriotic heart. Men of experience estimated the oil destroyed at 150,000 barrels.

Once they left the destruction of the oil field behind them, the Confederate column rode leisurely south until they reunited with Imboden on May 14 at Summersville. Imboden had chased the 91st Ohio Infantry and two companies of cavalry from the town during the evening of May 12, but Imboden's cavalry, commanded by his brother George, was able to capture the supply wagons belonging to the retreating Federal soldiers. Twenty-eight wagons filled with rations and supplies were a welcome addition to the scant food supplies that had been available to the Confederates for much of their march.

After a short period of rest, the soldiers of both columns made their way east through a wilderness area until they once again gained the relative safety of the Shenandoah

Valley. Jones and Imboden had achieved their purpose—and more.

As "Grumble" Jones reported to Lee:

In thirty days we marched nearly 700 miles [1,126km] through a rough and sterile country, gaining subsistence for man and horse by the way. At Greenland and Fairmont (and also at Bridgeport), we encountered enemy forces. We killed from 25 to 30 of the enemy, probably wounded three times as many, captured nearly 700 prisoners, with their small arms, and one piece of artillery, two trains of cars, burned 16 railroad bridges and one tunnel, 150,000 barrels of oil, many engines, and a large number of boats, tanks and barrels, bringing home with us about 1,000 cattle, and about 1,200 horses. Our entire loss was ten killed and 42 wounded, the missing not exceeding 15.

A very successful raid was concluded. Jones managed to divert large numbers of troops from their planned operations as the Union commanders scrambled to contain his movements. Fear was so great that two gunboats were sent up the Ohio River to Parkersburg to help contain Jones' regiments and prevent them from entering Ohio. Approximately twenty-five thousand Union troops were involved in actions designed to contain and engage Jones as he moved with relative impunity through western Virginia.

The Confederate commander's strategy of destroying the B&O at multiple points by burning bridges and destroying the tunnel made it difficult for Federal officers to concentrate their forces against Jones and Imboden at any single point. The additional tactic of dividing their men as they struck several targets simultaneously served to magnify their numbers in the view of their Union opponents. Reports of Jones' and Imboden's movements came from all quarters as panic only added false reports for the overall commander in the region, Benjamin F. Kelley, to consider.

Through leadership in the field and sheer audacity, Jones and Imboden had accomplished one of the boldest series of Confederate raids of the Civil War.

As the Union sought to counter the bold raids conducted by the Confederacy, Union cavalrymen began to appear in the field as Federal commanders. Cavalry units, with their speed and mobility, were best suited to such missions, and the Union army began to equip and deploy large cavalry elements to take on the Confederate raiders.

chapter

6

JOHN MORGAN RAIDS DEEPLY INTO THE UNION

Cavalry raids were lightning strikes that often went deep into enemy territory in support of a larger army movement. Used as a diversionary tactic and part of an overall strategy, these raids could throw an enemy into confusion at a time when he most needed information about the plans and intentions of his opponent.

This was true during the summer of 1863 in Tennessee when Confederate General Braxton Bragg found himself vulnerable to well-executed simultaneous strikes by William S. Rosecrans from the direction of Murfreesboro and by Ambrose E. Burnside from the Ohio River. These blows were to fall on a weakened Bragg, as many of his men had been sent to reinforce Vicksburg, which was besieged by Grant and in danger of capture. In order to avoid a dual attack,

Bragg planned to fall back, withdrawing his forces to the vicinity of Chattanooga.

Bragg planned to cover his withdrawal by ordering Brigadier General John Hunt Morgan, an experienced raider, out on a raid into Kentucky with orders to destroy railroads, strike isolated Federal units, and threaten Louisville. The plan was well conceived, but it didn't fit Morgan's own plan. He wanted to go deeper into Federal territory by striking across the Ohio River, but Bragg wouldn't give his permission for the longer raid.

John Morgan had other ideas and decided to defy Bragg, an intention he kept to himself. He departed on his expedition on July 2, during Robert E. Lee's Gettysburg campaign, but there were no plans within the Confederacy to attempt to coordinate this raid with Lee's movements at Gettysburg.

Morgan departed from Burkesville, Kentucky, with 2,460 selected men from Kentucky and Tennessee regiments, which were divided into two brigades. One was commanded by Colonel Basil W. Duke, Morgan's brother-in-law, and the second was led by Colonel Adam Johnson. Scouts had been sent ahead all along the route to the Ohio River, where Morgan hoped to cross and then reenter Confederate territory by riding across West Virginia. The region was still disrupted by the Jones-Imboden Raid, and since Federal units were still reeling and disorganized, Morgan felt that he could traverse the region safely.

Once they crossed the Cumberland River at Burkesville, they sped across Kentucky and terrified the residents of Louisville but made no attempt to enter the city. The men he sent forward captured two riverboats, which were used to transport the entire command across the Ohio River at Brandenburg on July 8. The crossing was opposed by a Federal gunboat and Home Guards with a cannon located on the Indiana side of the river, but all of Morgan's men were safely across by midnight. Morgan made sure that

PAGE 71: John Hunt Morgan became a hero to the Kentuckians who supported the Confederacy. After organizing his Kentucky Rifles, he and his men slipped away from Lexington as Kentucky's neutrality came to an end. He raided successfully far and wide, but his effectiveness lessened after he married in 1862. Disobeying orders, he crossed the Ohio River on his great raid, but landed in a Federal prison at its conclusion. LEFT: General Braxton Bragg had served ably as an officer in the Mexican War and he enjoyed some success in the western theater of operations during the Civil War. His audacious invasion of Kentucky in 1862 was coordinated with Lee's movement into Maryland, but Bragg's efforts were overshadowed by Lee's battle at Antietam. Later, Bragg fought well at Chickamauga, but a series of errors resulted in significant losses.

none of his men would begin to think of returning to Kentucky: he had the boats burned behind them. They rode deep into Indiana with Federal cavalry in pursuit as infantry and Home Guard units marched about in attempts to block the raiders. Both Indiana and Ohio were up in arms, and every move Morgan made had to account for local defense units as Union army cavalry brigades closed in on his rear. Detachments were sent out to burn bridges in attempts to delay pursuit, to confuse Union pursuers as to their actual course, and to magnify, as much as possible, their numbers.

The night of July 13, Morgan swung past Cincinnati, actually transiting the outskirts of the city, but did no real damage—other than cause the townspeople considerable emotional distress. By July 18, his lead elements had reached the Ohio River near Buffington Island, where he planned his crossing. Not only was the selected ford guarded by Union troops, but high water had made any attempt at crossing dangerous, even by daylight. With the cavalry brigades and infantry units closing in from the rear, Morgan chose to fight instead of surrender.

Dense fog covered the area at first daylight, and in the engagement that developed the Union forces were supported by two gunboats that began shelling Morgan's positions. Under intense pressure, the Confederates began to break and Morgan lost his wagons, artillery, and several hundred of his men, all of them captured along with his brother-in-law, Colonel Duke.

RIGHT: John Hunt Morgan's lightning-fast raids soon earned him the moniker "The Thunderbolt of the Confederacy," as Union forces were seldom able to predict where or when he would strike next. Careful scouting operations and well-planned, well-executed attacks made him one of the South's most feared raiders.

JOHN MORGAN RAIDS DEEPLY INTO THE UNION

RIGHT: Basil Duke, Morgan's brother-in-law, was an excellent officer and strategist who was invaluable to Morgan in the planning of his raids. After Duke was captured at the conclusion of their raid across Ohio, Morgan became increasingly ineffective. It became obvious to many observers that Duke had played a pivotal role in Morgan's operations.

MORGAN'S INDIANA AND OHIO RAID
July 2–26, 1863

1. On July 2 with 2,460 mounted troopers Morgan crossed the rain-swollen Cumberland River below Burkesville, Kentucky. After he brushed aside Union pickets that guarded the ford, he headed northward toward Columbia, Kentucky.

2. Union forces offered their first concentrated resistance near where Morgan had chosen to ford the Green River. Unable to dislodge the defenders, Morgan broke off the engagement, bypassed them, and headed toward Lebanon.

3. On July 8 Morgan crossed the Ohio River at Brandenburg in steamboats captured by his scouts the day before. Union pursuit forces arrived just as Morgan's rear guard crossed over the river.

4. At Corydon, Indiana, Morgan encountered and routed a force of 500 armed civilians. From this point on, Morgan was constantly ambushed by small groups of civilians and local militias.

5. On July 13 the raiders crossed over the Whitewater River into Ohio, and passed just to the north of Cincinnati.

6. On July 14 Morgan skirmished with a small force of ambulatory wounded Union soldiers at Camp Dennison, just east of Cincinnati. He then proceeded on to Williamsburg and rested his command for the first time since they entered Ohio.

7. A diversion and forage expedition led by Basil Duke split off from the main force of raiders and headed for the town of Ripley.

8. Union gunboats and pursuit forces attacked and captured many of Morgan's raiders as they attempted to cross the Ohio River at Buffington Island. Morgan and a few hundred raiders escaped the trap.

9. The surviving Raiders wandered west, then north through Ohio, toward Pennsylvania, clashing with Union pursuit forces and local militias.

10. Surrounded, Morgan and what was left of his command surrendered on July 26 near the town of Salineville, Ohio.

Morgan's raiders struck swiftly at their selected targets, like this attack on Washington, Ohio. The sudden appearance of Morgan's men struck terror into local defenders, who often fled or surrendered.

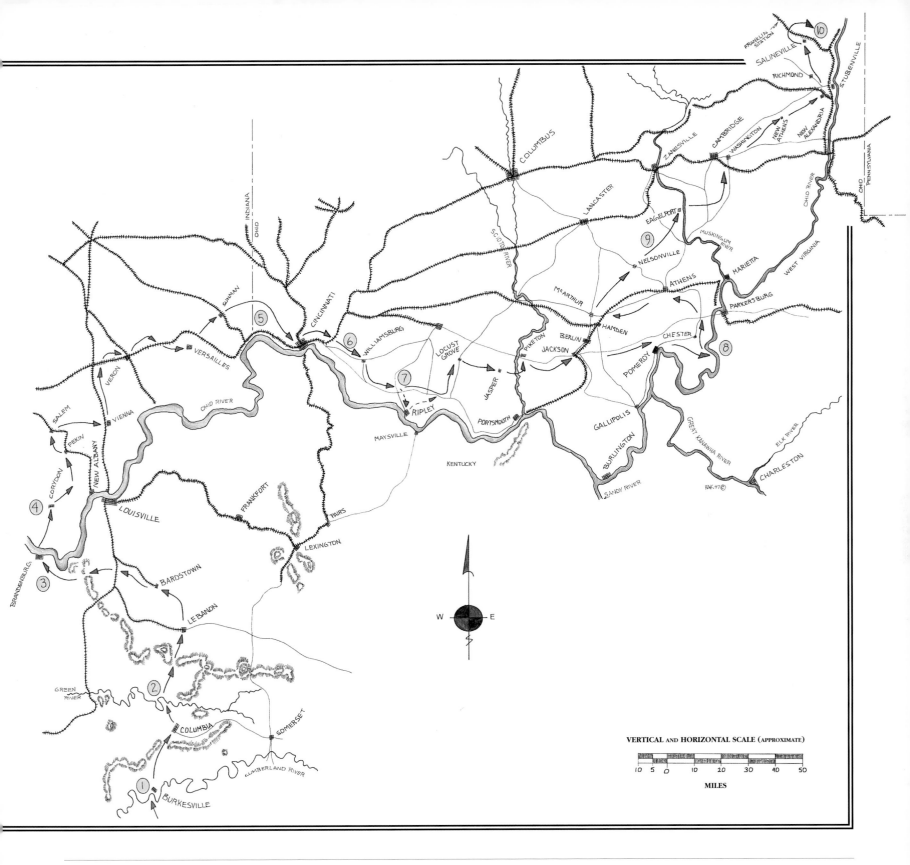

JOHN MORGAN RAIDS DEEPLY INTO THE UNION

75

JOHN MORGAN RAIDS DEEPLY INTO THE UNION

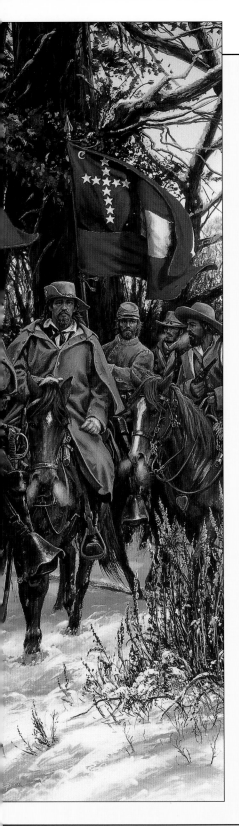

John Hunt Morgan's Career as a Raider

John Hunt Morgan gained his initial military experience during the Mexican War. Promoted to first lieutenant, he fought in the battle of Buena Vista. After the war, he returned to Kentucky, where he began a peacetime career as a businessman.

He had a successful career, but remained interested in military affairs. He organized the Kentucky Rifles in 1857, and they remained pro-Southern during the political crises that led to armed conflict. As Kentucky's attempts to remain neutral began to fail, he and his men slipped away from Lexington to join up with the Confederate army near Bowling Green, Kentucky, on September 20, 1861. They were forced to withdraw from Kentucky in early February, and Morgan was promoted to full colonel as a result of the raids he had led

John Hunt Morgan was an effective and courageous leader, but it is doubtful that he would have performed as well without the guidance of his brother-in-law, Basil Duke (marching beside him, at left) and his uncle, Thomas W. Hunt (behind him). The trio is depicted here leading over one thousand troops though the snow-covered hills of Tennessee in December 1862.

behind Federal lines. Morgan was a skilled raider who was in command of a group of brave, skillful riders, led by himself and disciplined by Basil W. Duke, his brother-in-law and second-in-command. The two men complemented each other—each supplied what was lacking in the other. They became expert at the hit-and-run tactics typical of the Confederate raiders.

Morgan's men included some flamboyant characters, like his wiretap specialist, George "Lightning" Ellsworth, who tapped into Union telegraph lines to gain intelligence on their plans, and George St. Leger Grenfell, a British soldier of fortune who soon became one of Morgan's favorites. Another of his men was Champ Furguson, a Kentucky guerrilla who had developed a habit of killing Union prisoners—a practice Morgan made him promise to discontinue before allowing him to join his force.

Morgan and his men were at Shiloh on April 6–7, 1862, and Morgan assisted with rear guard actions at the end of the battle. This was the only major battle in which he directly participated, but he developed his 2nd Kentucky Cavalry Regiment into an excellent raiding force. He was soon to use it at Tompkinsville on July 9, 1862, where he reported:

I was aware that a considerable body of cavalry, about 380 or 400 strong, were stationed at this town, and I thought by a rapid night march I might succeed in surprising them. I left the river at 10 P.M. on the 8th instant, and at 5 A.M. this day I surprised the enemy, and having surrounded them, threw four shells into their camp, and then carried it by a dashing charge. The enemy fled, leaving about 22 dead and 30 to 40 wounded in our hands. We have 30 prisoners and my Texas squadron are still in pursuit of the fugitives. Among the prisoners is Major Jordan, their commander, and two lieutenants. The tents, stores, and camp equipage I have destroyed, but a valuable baggage train, consisting of some 20 wagons and 50 mules, is in my possession; also some 40 cavalry horses, and supplies of sugar, coffee, &c. I did not lose a single man killed, but have to regret that Colonel Hunt, while leading a brilliant charge, received a severe wound in the leg.... I also had three members of the Texas squadron wounded, but not seriously.

He continued with his raiding in the region, reaching the telegraph line along the Louisville & Nashville north of Tompkinsville, where he tapped the telegraph line. "Lightning" Ellsworth sent out a flurry of phony messages. The messages alerted commanders throughout the Ohio Valley and produced panic in both Louisville and Cincinnati, potential targets of the raiders. Morgan kept the pressure on by riding swiftly to the banks of the Ohio River between Louisville and Cincinnati.

On July 17, Morgan struck at a lightly defended Federal depot in the town of Cynthiana, south of Cincinnati, and captured or drove off the defenders as frightened Federal commanders fired off messages in all directions requesting reinforcements. Morgan was on his way back to the safety of Tennessee before any reinforcements arrived. The results of the raid were impressive: Morgan's raiders had covered over 1,000 miles (1,609km) in three weeks, and captured 1,200 prisoners and seventeen towns as he delayed the Union army advance against Chattanooga.

He led another raid as a part of Braxton Bragg's invasion in late summer 1862. On August 12, Morgan captured the garrison at Gallatin, Tennessee, and burned the depot and train trestles before pushing wagons filled with hay into a long tunnel. The burning hay ignited the supporting timbers within the tunnel, cracked rocks, and caused the tunnel to collapse—creating a barrier that would require a major effort to clear.

Morgan missed the culminating battle of Bragg's campaign at Perryville, Kentucky, on October 8, 1862, as a tactical stalemate developed and Bragg was forced by his heavy casualties to retreat. The grand strategy of bringing Kentucky into the Confederacy by force was dropped after Perryville. Morgan moved back through Kentucky independently of Bragg's retreating army, but he was back in the field once again by December.

His command had been assigned to disrupt the Federal supply lines between Louisville and Nashville and he once again set off on an independent raid. After a grim winter march, Morgan and his troopers—with an infantry element attached—struck hard at the Federal defenders, two thousand strong, at Hartsville, and captured the entire garrison.

John Morgan married a seventeen-year-old beauty on December 12, the day after he was promoted to the rank of brigadier general, and the aggressive commander was off on another two-week raid into Kentucky. He struck hard at the Louisville & Nashville Railroad, destroying miles of track and millions of dollars worth of military supplies and capturing nearly two thousand prisoners.

At this time in his military career, however, his leadership ability began to be questioned. Once he was wed to the beautiful Mattie Ready, his attention was clearly distracted from military operations. He actually disobeyed his orders when he embarked on his great raid across Ohio, which landed him in the Ohio Penitentiary, but he and seven of his officers managed a spectacular escape on November 27, 1863, and he returned to duty.

Morgan's reputation had been severely damaged following that raid, which nearly destroyed his entire command. He quickly set off on another raid, this time into nearby Kentucky in an attempt to salvage what was left of his military career. Some of his men plundered private property during this raid and Morgan minimized their actions. Basil Duke was still in prison, and Morgan missed the excellent advice he had received from his brother-in-law and advisor in the past. His tendency to disobey orders began to alarm his superiors.

He attacked successfully once again at Cynthiana, Kentucky, on June 11, 1864, where he captured the 600 Federal defenders, but he broke the cardinal rule of the successful raider by remaining at the site of his attack overnight. Having time to react to his presence, a large Union force struck Morgan the next day, and he suffered severe casualties. He was soon transferred to command in eastern Tennessee and western Virginia, but the charges by his superior officers continued and Morgan was relieved of his duties on August 22, 1864.

Characteristically, Morgan ignored the order that relieved him and on his own led his men against a large Union force moving toward his positions. He was killed at Greenville, Tennessee, on September 4, 1864—one week before a court of inquiry was to convene to review his suspension.

OPPOSITE: Having lost his first wife just before going off to war, Morgan was attracted to the lovely Mattie Ready of Murfreesboro. After they were married in December 1862, Morgan's effectiveness as a combat commander began to decline. Many people attributed this to the distraction provided by his lovely new wife, although it is equally likely that his performance was affected by the departure of his brother-in-law and advisor, Basil Duke.

JOHN MORGAN RAIDS DEEPLY INTO THE UNION

JOHN MORGAN RAIDS DEEPLY INTO THE UNION

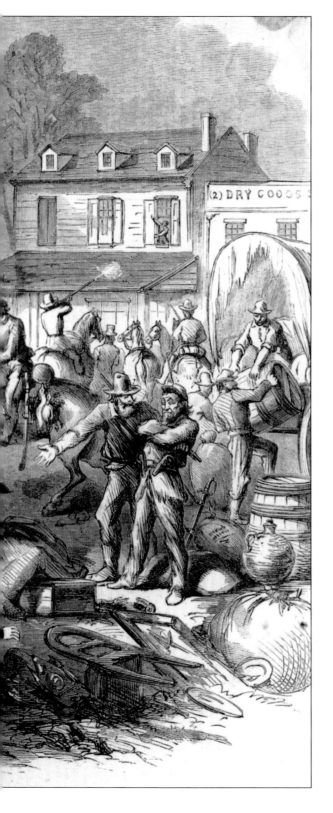

Colonel Johnson and many of the men of his brigade were able to escape from the trap between the Union army on one side and the swollen Ohio River on the other. After an eighteen-mile (29km) ride upstream, they attempted to swim their mounts across to West Virginia; 280 men arrived safely. Several men drowned in the attempt to reach the shore, and General Morgan was in the middle of the stream when the arrival of a gunboat and its shelling forced him to return to the Ohio side of the river.

Johnson and the few survivors who made it across the Ohio River were helped by Confederate sympathizers along the river, but the arrival of West Virginia troops in the area forced them to move quickly into the interior of the new state. They evaded any further contact with Union troops in the area and were able to slowly cross the area to enter the safety of eastern Virginia.

Morgan and the survivors of the fight at Buffington Island were able to evade capture, but each day more men were lost. After a full week, Morgan and the rest of his men surrendered near East Liverpool, Ohio. He had led the Union army on quite a chase, but in the end, he lost most of his command without having accomplished a great deal.

Morgan was imprisoned in the Ohio Penitentiary at Columbus, along with sixty-eight officers from his command. On November 27, he and seven of his officers were able to escape from their cell through a tunnel they had laboriously dug over a period of twenty days with two small knives. After escaping, they separated and Morgan and Captain Thomas H. Hines calmly boarded a train in Columbus for Cincinnati, where they crossed into Kentucky. By December 5, Morgan and Hines were back in the vicinity of Burkesville and soon were able to link up with a part of Morgan's command that had not taken part in the disastrous raid. They crossed into Tennessee on December 13 but

OPPOSITE: Union newspapers and periodicals often carried illustrations of wartime events, such as this one titled "John Morgan's highwaymen sacking a peaceful village in the West," published in 1862. Such propaganda resulted in hardened attitudes toward Confederates, and captured raiders were normally condemned to state prisons—as were Morgan and those of his men who survived the raid across Ohio. ABOVE: Bold John Hunt Morgan was a cavalier from Kentucky's Bluegrass region. Quickly deciding to cast his lot with the Confederacy, Morgan embarked on a career as a dashing and successful raider. Unfortunately, he lacked the ability to accept the degree of supervision required to conduct large, coordinated campaigns, and his daring raid across Ohio ended in disaster.

had to continue to evade Federal cavalry patrols, one of which recaptured the unfortunate Captain Hines.

Morgan was back in the Confederacy, but he was given no command until April 1864. He lost his life in a clash with Union forces on September 4, 1864, while on an expedition into the interior of Tennessee.

chapter
7

JOHN MCCAUSLAND BURNS A PENNSYLVANIA TOWN

"Should guerrillas or bushwhackers molest our march, or should the inhabitants burn bridges, obstruct roads, or otherwise manifest hostility, then army commanders should order and enforce a devastation more or less relentless."

—*General William T. Sherman*

s the Union casualty lists from combat during the first three years of the war grew, anger and the desire to inflict punishment on the South grew also, along with resentment for their "great crime" of secession. This became especially true in the Shenandoah Valley of Virginia, where Federal invasions had been met by Confederate armies while "bushwhackers" and "guerrillas" attacked the rear areas of the Union commands. Captured and forced to take an oath of loyalty to the Union on their release, the guerrillas nonetheless usually returned to their partisan warfare. Gradually the Union army began to develop a merciless attitude toward them and their supporters. By 1864 it was common for Federal patrols to set fire to any property of secessionists found in the immediate vicinity of a bushwhacking attack. Cruelty was matched by cruelty, and the violence worsened as raid was followed by reprisal.

One of the most relentless of the Federal commanders—at least where the destruction of civilian property was concerned—was General David Hunter, a Virginian who chose to remain loyal to the Union. He was placed in command of the Shenandoah Valley after Major General Franz Sigel was defeated at New Market, and Hunter took his duties and orders quite seriously. On July 17, he received a message from the Union army's chief of staff, General Henry Halleck, that changed the focus of the war considerably.

Hunter's own chief of staff, David Hunter Strother, wrote in his diary:

July 17, Sunday....Received a telegram from General Halleck informing

General Hunter....He was to devastate the valleys south of the railroad as far as possible so that crows flying over would have to carry knapsacks. This need not involve the burning of houses, dwellings. I have begged off Charles Town being burnt for the third time.

Strothel wrote of the following two days:

July 18, Monday....The house of Andrew Hunter was burned yesterday by Martindale. I am sorry to see this warfare begin and would be glad to stop it, but I don't pity the individuals at all. A war of mutual devastation will depopulate the border counties which contain all my kindred on both sides of the question. I would fain save them but fear all will go under alike in the end.

July 19, Tuesday....Orders given to burn the houses of E.J. Lee and Alex. Boteler. Martindale went forward to execute it. His description of the women and the scene is heart-rending.

PAGE 83: Brigadier General John McCausland had served at the Virginia Military Institute, where he taught mathematics under Thomas J. Jackson, later to be known as "Stonewall." As the war opened, young McCausland was ordered to western Virginia to recruit men to defend the state's border with Ohio. Later, he would be assigned the command of a cavalry brigade, and with this, he was able to delay the Union attack on Lynchburg—winning a golden sword and silver spurs from the city's grateful citizens. He received less welcome treatment at the hands of the Union army once he ordered the burning of Chambersburg. LEFT: The Civil War took a dramatic turn toward unrestrained violence during the campaign of spring 1864. Henry Halleck, the Union army's chief-of-staff, sent orders to his commander in the Shenandoah Valley, David Hunter, to begin the devastation of the region. His cruelty provoked fierce reprisals, and a cycle of barely restrained violence began to emerge.

David Hunter, known as "Black Dave" even to his own men, had been back in the region as commander only since July 15. In that short period of time, the face of warfare in the Shenandoah region began to change considerably. David Strother had been correct: a war of mutual devastation was about to begin. The local Confederate commander was Jubal Early, a man who would not stand for the destruction of civilian property without ordering a response.

Brigadier General John McCausland, a Confederate cavalry commander from West Virginia, was assigned to Early's command, and he later described a dispatch he received from Jubal Early: "I opened it and when I read those first lines I nearly fell out of the saddle. He ordered me in a very few words to make a retaliatory raid and give the Yankees a taste of their own medicine."

John McCausland, an aggressive officer still in his twenties at this time, was himself called "Tiger John" by his men. He was an experienced opponent of Hunter as he had managed to keep his small cavalry brigade in front of Hunter's invading army after "Grumble" Jones' blocking force was defeated in the battle of Piedmont. With the death of Jones, the way was cleared for Hunter to strike deep into central Virginia. He selected the industrial city of Lynchburg as his target, but McCausland was able to delay his progress through an extended series of hit-and-run attacks that began to deplete Hunter's army of both food and ammunition.

David Hunter, known as "Black Dave" even to his own men, responded to Halleck's orders to begin the destruction of the Shenandoah Valley area with ferocious enthusiasm. Having lost in his attack on Lynchburg—primarily due to the unrelenting efforts of John McCausland—Hunter reappeared in the region after Early's unsuccessful attack on Washington and renewed his old habit of burning dwellings that had no military significance.

Once Early was able to reinforce the doomed town's garrison, Hunter was forced to flee into the isolated mountains of southern West Virginia, where his men began to starve and were hit by repeated attacks by local Partisan Rangers.

McCausland was presented with a gold-inlaid sword and a pair of silver spurs by the grateful citizens of Lynchburg for saving the town, and Early was able to begin a long march back down the Shenandoah Valley along the route taken toward Lynchburg by Hunter. Hunter's retreat into southern West Virginia left the entire Shenandoah Valley without Federal defenders, and Early, quick to take advantages, marched confidently into the power vacuum.

Soon he and his small army were fighting at Monocacy, Virginia, only a short march from the defenses of Washington, D.C. Had it not been for the spirited delaying action fought that day by Union General Lew Wallace, it is quite likely that the North's capital city would have been captured, even if only briefly, during an election year when the Northern Democrats had nominated a peace candidate, former general George Brinton McClellan.

During this attack, McCausland led the advancing army and managed to enter the defensive works at Georgetown. He came closer to the Washington Monument than any other Confederate officer during the war.

Union General Lew Wallace ensured a Union victory for Grant at Fort Donelson in 1863 as he rapidly moved his division to contain an aggressive Confederate breakout attempt led by John McCausland. Wallace probably saved Washington, D.C. (and Lincoln's re-election) when he protected the city from occupation by Jubal Early's small army during the summer of 1864. During his successful defense against Early at the battle of Monocacy, Wallace was attacked by John McCausland. Lew Wallace later authored the classic novel, **Ben Hur.**

JOHN McCAUSLAND BURNS A PENNSYLVANIA TOWN

The small town of Chambersburg, Pennsylvania, with its gaslights burning, must have shone like a gleaming jewel as McCausland's men rode within sight. It was immediately occupied, and calls for the leading citizens of the town to assemble went out, but they refused to comply with the ransom order, either having sent much of the town's money to safety or relying on the nearby presence of Averell's cavalry division to save them from Early's terrible order.

Early decided to mount a reprisal expedition, and chose McCausland, a fighting general, to head it.

In his *Memoirs,* published after the war, Early wrote:

> *The town of Chambersburg in Pennsylvania was selected as the one on which retaliation should be made, and McCausland was ordered to proceed, with his brigade and that of Johnson and a battery of artillery, to that place, and demand of the municipal authorities the sum of $100,000 in gold or $500,000 in U.S. currency, as a compensation for the destruction of the houses named and their contents; and in default of that payment, to lay the town in ashes. A written demand to that effect was sent to the authorities, and they were informed what would be the result of a failure or refusal to comply with it; for I desired to give the people of Chambersburg an opportunity of saving their town, by making compensation for part of the injury done, and hoped the payment of a sum would have the effect of causing the adoption of a different policy.*

The two cavalry brigades and the artillery battery that would make the raid were prepared swiftly, and they began their long march northward on July 28. McCausland estimated the distance from the closest Confederate territory, Martinsburg, to Chambersburg to be seventy miles (113km). The cavalry crossed it quickly and arrived on the hills overlooking Chambersburg in the early hours of July 30, 1864.

Chambersburg would have appeared lovely from those hilltops in the early morning as darkness was setting. The relatively wealthy town had gaslit streets and was visible from some distance at night. The town's citizens would have been sleeping peacefully, under the impression that they were safe. Although the town had been occupied twice during the war up to the that point, it had sustained only minimal damage.

The war was about to touch the sleepy town in an entirely unfamiliar way, however: hard men were approaching to extort a ransom from the townspeople. Other Maryland towns had recently paid for their safety: Frederick had paid Early $200,000 following the successful conclusion of the battle of Monocacy, with the shrewd city fathers delaying payment until it was decided who would win the battle. Prior to this, Early had dispatched John McCausland to capture Hagerstown with verbal orders to collect $200,000 there as well.

McCausland returned with $20,000 and some supplies, and is reported by several historians to have erroneously dropped a decimal point, but the former mathematics professor was unlikely to have made such an error. It is more likely that McCausland decided not to burn Hagerstown for its lack of financial support for the Confederacy, and that he experienced a severe dressing-down from Early for his humanity. With Chambersburg, there would be no mathematical or judgemental misunderstanding

John McCausland Burns a Pennsylvania Town

between them: Early gave McCausland written orders that contained no latitude for interpretation, and the town was doomed unless it paid the demanded ransom.

A member of the raiding party, Fielder Slingluff, wrote an article based on a letter he had written to a Chambersburg resident at the time of the raid. In part, he wrote:

...you would like to know if the men...justified the burning of your town, in their individual capacity, irrespective of the orders from headquarters under which they acted. I must say to you frankly that they did, and I never heard one dissenting voice. And why did we justify so harsh a measure? Simply because we had long come to the conclusion that it was time to burn something in the enemy's country. In the campaign of the preceding year, when our whole army had passed through your richest section of country, where the peaceful homes and fruitful fields only made the contrast with what he had left the more significant, many a man whose home was in ruins chaffed under the orders from General Lee, which forbade him to touch them, but the orders were obeyed, and we left the homes and fields as we found them, the ordinary wear and tear of an army of occupation excepted. We had so often in our eyes the reverse of this wherever your army swept through Virginia, that we were thoroughly convinced of the justice of stern retaliation.

The twenty-eight-year-old McCausland had been ordered to collect $100,000 in gold or $500,000 in Union "greenbacks"—illustrating the inflated value of paper money at that point in the war. Chambersburg was prosperous, and the townspeople might well have been able to pay the ransom that would have saved their town, but they chose to defy the threat.

It is no pleasure to me to recall the scenes of those days, nor do I do so in any spirit of vindictiveness, but I simply tell the truth in justification. We had followed Kilpatrick (I think it was), in his raid through Madison, Greene and other counties, and had seen the cattle shot or hamstrung in the barnyards, the agricultural implements burned, the feather beds and clothing of the women and children cut in shreds in mere wantonness, farmhouse after farmhouse stripped of every particle of provisions, private carriages cut and broken up, and women in tears lamenting all this. I did not put down anything I did not see myself. We had seen a thousand ruined homes in Clark, Jefferson and Frederick counties—barns and houses burned and private property destroyed—but we had no knowledge that this was done by "Official Orders." At last when the official order came openly from General Hunter, and the burning done thereunder, and when our orders of retaliation came they were met with approbation, as I have said, of every man who crossed the Potomac to execute them.

Of course we had nothing personal against your pretty little town. It just happened that it was the nearest and most accessible place of importance for us to get to. It was the unfortunate victim of circumstances. Had it been further off and some other town nearer that other town would have gone and Chambersburg would have been spared.

As it was, the town had several opportunities to save itself. McCausland sent a copy of the written demand into the town and rode there to personally request that the ransom be paid. Slingluff wrote of the response McCausland received: "They treated it as a

The destruction of Chambersburg was nearly total as flames consumed almost nearly three-quarters of the entire town. There was no military advantage to be gained by the burning, and McCausland was soon indicted for arson—a charge he felt was entirely unfair, as Sheridan and Sherman were burning far more than a single town.

JOHN MCCAUSLAND BURNS A PENNSYLVANIA TOWN

When Confederate cavalry rode into the "Diamond," Chambersburg's town square, on July 20, 1864, they intended to ride out with the ransom demanded by Jubal Early. The Confederate soldiers had also witnessed the "heart-rending scenes" described by Early as his army retraced the route taken by "Black Dave" Hunter. They were in the mood to burn something, and Chambersburg had the misfortune to be the first town they encountered.

joke, or thought it was a mere threat to get the money, and showed their sense of security and incredulity in every act."

The townspeople had good reason to feel that they were secure. General William W. Averell's combat-experienced cavalry division had arrived at Greencastle and was only ten miles (16km) away as McCausland delivered his ransom demands. McCausland was also aware of Averell's presence, as one of the Union commander's men had been captured. McCausland, however, was also aware that he had only a limited period of time before Averell's hardened troopers would be charging over the nearby hills.

McCausland actually went into the Diamond, as the town square was called, and approached at least one citizen, Mr. W. Douglas. Douglas wrote:

He took me by the arm, and leading me out into the Diamond, said: "Are you sure you have not seen your public men? I should be very sorry to carry out the retributive part of the command of my superior officer." And as we walked to the Court House, he said: "Can't you ring the Court House bell and call the citizens together and see if this sum of money cannot be raised?"...He then ordered some of his men to open the Court House with the butts of their muskets and ring the bell. Then several of our citizens came and engaged in conversation with General McCausland, when I left, going to my hotel to notify my mother of the coming storm and save some articles of value to no one but family.

The threat of Averell's arrival combined with the uneventful previous occupations of the town and the fact that most of the available money was in the local banks doomed the town. As well, the general attitude of the town's citizens did little to endear them to

their temporary occupiers, who were called "Damned Rebs" and ordered to get out of town. One member of the town council said that the citizens wouldn't pay five cents! Their fate was sealed.

Details were sent into the middle of the town and fires were set. In a few minutes, the courthouse and the town hall were both in flames and the fire began to spread rapidly. The main portion of the town was enveloped in flames within ten minutes. The horrific scene was described by J. Scott Moore, one of the cavalrymen present:

The conflagration at its height was one of surpassing grandeur and terror, and had the day not been a calm one, many would have been licked up by the flames in the streets. Tall, black columns of smoke rose up to the very skies; around it were wrapped long streams of flames, writhing and twisting themselves into a thousand fantas-

tic shapes. Here and there gigantic whirlwinds would lift clothing and light substances into the air, and intermingled with the weird scene could be heard the shrieks of women and children. Cows, dogs and cats were consumed in their attempt to escape. It was a picture that may be misrepresented, but cannot be heightened, and must remain forever indelibly upon the minds of those who witnessed it.

Three-fourths of the town was destroyed in the huge conflagration. One section was spared when officer Colonel William Peters refused to set it aflame. He was later arrested, but returned to his regiment at Moorefield a few days later.

There were remarkably few deaths during the raid and the burning of the town. Daniel Parker, an elderly former slave (he "filled the measure of patriarchal years,"

OPPOSITE: William Woods Averell had proven himself to be an effective raider, but he was severely criticized after the burning of Chambersburg. Camped only ten miles (16 km) away, Averell didn't ride to save the town. He may have been arranging a massive ambush, but, regardless, most historians agree that he should be excused of blame: there had been no burnings on Union soil up to this point in the war, and he had no way to anticipate that Chambersburg was in mortal danger. He would, however, avenge Chambersburg with his surprise attack on McCausland's entire command at Moorefield, West Virginia. RIGHT: Confederate General Jubal Early, the commander in the Shenandoah region, began to receive appeals for assistance that were, as he described them, "truly heart-rending" and he ordered a retaliatory attack. Having successfully extorted a ransom from Frederick, Maryland, and a small ransom—through error only $20,000 instead of $200,000—from Hagerstown, Early ordered a raid into Pennsylvania. John McCausland was ordered to collect a ransom from the citizens of Chambersburg to pay for damages done by Union raiders or he was to burn the entire town.

JOHN McCAUSLAND BURNS A PENNSYLVANIA TOWN

according to newspapers reporting the destruction), died as a result of the raid. Two Union soldiers were shot to death in a drugstore by the enraged owner. Two Confederate officers lost their lives. One, Calder Bailey, was drinking heavily and was left behind; an enraged mob shot and wounded him, forcing him to take refuge in the cellar of a burning building; when he emerged to escape from the blistering heat, he was beaten to death with clubs.

The other Confederate officer, Henry K. Cochrane, was captured by Thomas H. Doyle, who gave his prisoner fifteen minutes to pray before shooting him. This nonjudicial execution and the killing of Bailey were widely reported in the North, where the population accepted the acts, essentially murders of prisoners, without question. Chambersburg was as legitimate a military target as were the homes and farms in the Shenandoah Valley that were being burned, but the Northern population viewed the two acts differently: burnings in the South were acts of reprisal designed to punish their Southern cousins for the crime of secession, but the destruction of Chambersburg was viewed as an act of arson done by criminal elements.

The raiders withdrew slowly from the area, probably wondering why they hadn't been attacked by the nearby Averell and his cavalry division. Averell was an unusual commander and a complex character, who was capable of valiant efforts, but seemed to "run both hot and cold" at times. He had led the winter attack all the way across West Virginia's mountains to strike deep in the Confederacy's rear areas, but he was also capable of indecisiveness at times, a fact that

OPPOSITE: The destruction in Chambersburg was nearly total, but only one citizen lost his life, an elderly black man who may have suffered a heart attack. Unfortunately, history has made light of the nonjudicial executions of captured Confederates from the raiding force.

would limit his military career in only a few months. Several attempts to contact Averell were made, and he was found sleeping beside a fence line. While he was only ten miles (16km) from the doomed town, Averell did not ride to the rescue.

In fairness to Averell, he and his cavalry division had just arrived in the area after a season of extremely hard marching and fighting. He had fought McCausland and had developed respect for the fighting ability of the west Virginian and his men. Averell wrote of the campaign he had just completed: "This command has marched 1,400 miles [2,253km] since the 1st of May, without a remount, and without a halt sufficiently long to set the shoes on my horses."

While resting his command, Averell must have believed that McCausland would occupy Chambersburg only temporarily before evacuating the town and retreating back along rural roads to rejoin Early's army near Martinsburg. There is no way Averell would have suspected that Early had ordered the town burned, as the Southern army, unlike the Union army, had never burned anything prior to this.

McCausland's force retreated rapidly from the town. Soon thereafter in Hancock, Maryland, McCausland demanded an additional ransom of $30,000, but the Maryland contingent with his command assigned guards to each building in the town to prevent burning or looting. They continued on to the federal garrison town of Cumberland, Maryland, where the commander, General Benjamin F. Kelley, prepared to meet him. McCausland ordered his men forward in an attack, but with heavy resistance in his front and Averell's cavalry riding toward his rear, the Confederate commander was forced to cross the Potomac and ride for the relative safety of the mountainous region.

McCausland continued to fight as his men rode. They destroyed a bridge in the

"I have the best possible reason for knowing the strength of the Confederate army to be one million men, for whenever one of our generals engages a rebel army he reports that he has encountered a force twice his strength. Now I know we have a half a million soldiers, so I am bound to believe that the rebels have twice that number."

—President Abraham Lincoln, 1862

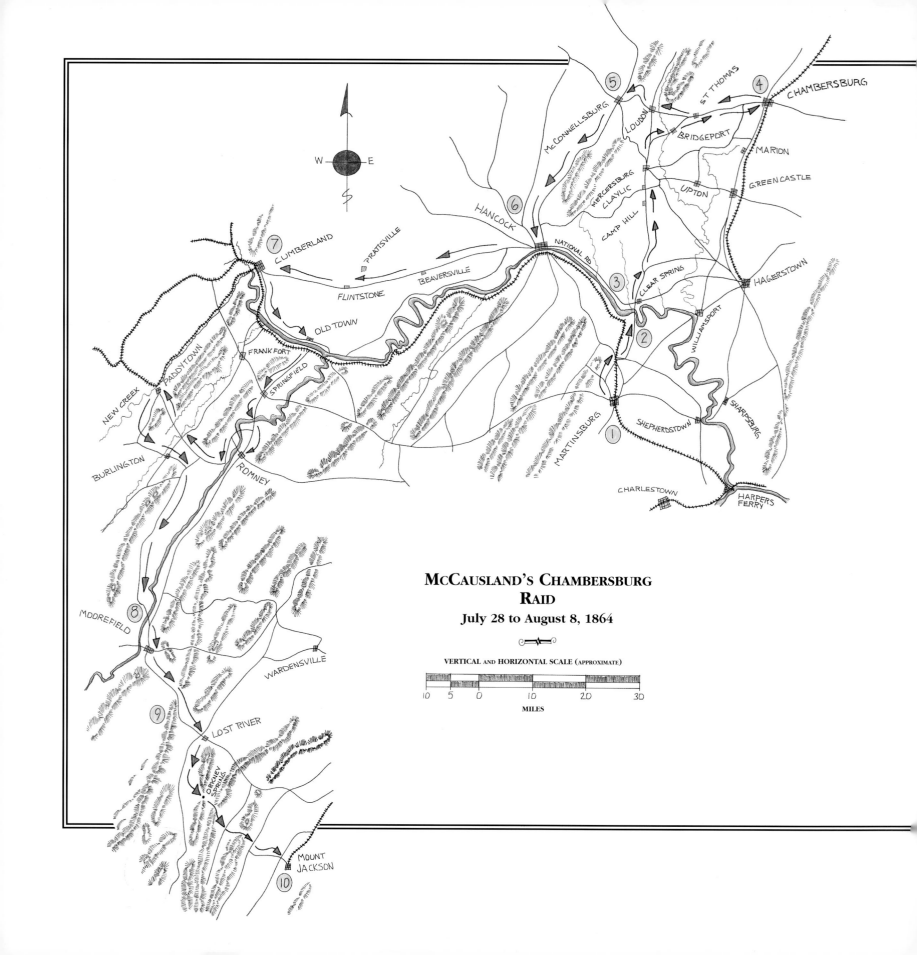

McCausland's Chambersburg RAID

July 28 to August 8, 1864

VERTICAL AND HORIZONTAL SCALE (APPROXIMATE)

10 5 0 10 20 30

MILES

1. On July 28, 1864, McCausland departed Martinsburg, West Virginia, with two brigades of artillery. His destination was Chambersburg, Pennsylvania; his orders were to collect monetary restitutions for Union raids in the Shenandoah Valley or burn the town.

2. At first light on July 29, Confederate scouts, who were pre-positioned the night before, surprised and captured Union pickets at McCoy's Ford on the Potomac. With the ford secured, McCausland's main body crossed over.

3. When the raiders reached the National Road, McCausland sent scouts toward Cumberland and Hagerstown to drive back Union pickets and to mask his real destination. McCausland passed through Clear Springs and headed north on the road to Mercersburg, en route to Chambersburg.

4. Early on July 30, McCausland arrived at the outskirts of Chambersburg. The town was secured with very little opposition. When the ransom was not met, McCausland ordered the town burned.

5. The raiders camped over night at the town of McConnellsburg.

6. On July 31, the raiders stopped again to rest at Hancock, Maryland. An attempt was made to collect a ransom, but before the money could be raised, Union forces attacked Confederate picket posts outside of town. After a lively fight, McCausland moved toward Cumberland by the National Road.

7. McCausland attacked Union infantry that blocked his way at Cumberland. When pursuit forces approached from Hancock, McCausland disengaged and headed south to Old Town, where he re-crossed the Potomac.

8. On August 7, Union pursuit forces caught up with McCausland as he rested at Moorefield. Union cavalry dressed in Confederate uniforms, known as "Jessie Scouts," rode directly into McCausland's camp and opened fire. At the same time, regular Union cavalry attacked down the road from Romney.

9. Fragmented after their defeat at Moorefield, McCausland's remaining troopers traveled on separate roads as they made their way southeast to Mount Jackson.

10. On August 8, the remnants of McCausland's command reached Mount Jackson.

vicinity of Romney and ordered an attack against the Union garrison at New Creek, Averell's former base of operations. The defenders lost seventy-five men before McCausland ordered his men to retire in the direction of Moorefield.

The Confederates had ridden sixty miles (96.5km) since they last encountered Averell's advance units at Hancock, and they went into camp for four days to rest and recuperate after the mind-numbing ride they had just experienced. Scout reports told of Averell doing the same thing in the vicinity of Hancock and the men began to relax.

McCausland's scouts, left along the Romney road, began to report the movement of Averell's men into the area and told McCausland that he could anticipate an attack at daylight on August 7. A warning was sent to the commander of the Maryland brigade, Bradley Johnson; orders were sent to at least a part of his command to prepare their mounts for quick use, and a patrol was sent out in the night. Unfortunately, no warning of the probable approach of Averell was given to subordinate commanders, and many of those weary officers returned to their blankets.

Averell used his Jessie Scouts, the gray-clad riders who had been instrumental in the success of his winter raid against the Confederate depot at Salem. These men managed to capture both the patrol ordered out on the Romney road by Johnson and the Confederate advance pickets—without a shot being fired. After learning the password, the location of the picket reserve, and the name of the picket reserve's commanding officer, these same scouts, reinforced by volunteer cavalrymen also wearing Confederate uni-

forms, rode to the picket post, calling, "Lieutenant Bonn, you are relieved." This was the command that they were awaiting, but they soon found themselves taken prisoner; still not a shot had been fired.

As the prisoners were taken to the rear, the disguised Federal patrol rode directly to the perimeter of Bradley Johnson's brigade camp and, pretending to be the returning patrol sent out earlier on the Romney road, entered. One group rode directly to the McNeil home, where Johnson was sleeping, while another rode into the center of the perimeter, searching for Harry Gilmor. They began shooting from within the interior of the Confederate camp—while wearing gray uniforms—and as complete confusion developed among the Confederates, Averell ordered a general attack against Johnson.

Hit suddenly by an entire Federal division of cavalry while their commander was being routed out of his bed inside the McNeil home, the Confederates were rapidly overrun as Averell's men continued their charge to the fords of the South Branch of the Potomac and the location where McCausland's brigade was encamped. Only hard fighting at the fords saved McCausland from complete destruction as small groups of Confederate cavalrymen galloped to what safety they could find on their own.

Chambersburg had been avenged by a cavalry charge that was the greatest surprise attack in the history of the North American continent, a charge that had been set up by the actions of a unique group of scouts. These men would be involved in additional daring operations against the Confederacy as the Union army continued to develop into a highly trained fighting force.

chapter

8

Jessie Scouts Capture Harry Gilmor

Hanse McNeil was one of the Confederacy's most ingenious partisan leaders. He had been a successful farmer and livestock breeder who entered the service of Virginia even though he was personally opposed to secession. He was living in Missouri at the outbreak of the war and was soon captured, but after escaping he returned to the vicinity of Moorefield, Virginia, where he raised a Partisan Ranger company and began to conduct operations against the nearby Baltimore and Ohio Railroad, the most vulnerable of the Union's supply arteries. Most of its rails ran through Virginia, and its trains, filled with supplies, coal, and troops, were often attacked by Virginia's raiders.

McNeil learned a great deal about the psychology of the young Union soldiers who were sent out in small groups to guard critical points along the railroad. In one attack, he called out to the young Federal soldiers that he would parole every man who surrendered and they could go home. The tactic, surprising as it was, worked, and McNeil's twenty-four men captured seventy-two Union troops. He began to use this tactic in a more wholesale way: he left signed parole forms with local farmers, and any Union soldier who wanted to go home could simply trade for one of the forms, complete it, and depart for home and family until exchanged.

As the spring campaign began in 1864, McNeil became more than simply an irritant to Benjamin F. Kelley, the local Federal commander, the unfortunate man responsible for the safety of the railroad. On May 3, McNeil and sixty of his men climbed aboard a train that had been stopped, placed a pistol to the

PAGE 99: *Major Harry Gilmor slipped across the Potomac River from Maryland on August 30, 1861, and joined Turner Ashby's Virginia cavalry. He served as a scout during Jackson's incredible 1862 Shenandoah Valley campaigns, but he best served the Confederacy as a raider with an independent command. Gilmor was one of those rare officers who seemed to thrive on leading his men into combat. ABOVE: Gilmor's nemesis throughout the latter part of the war came in the form of Jessie Scouts, Union soldiers wearing Confederate uniforms as they searched for Confederates. Gilmor knew a great deal about Jessie Scout operations and organized hunts for these daring Federal soldiers. One of the best of the Jessie scouts was Archibald Rowand, pictured here with a group of Medal of Honor winners. Rowand is in the back row at the far right.*

head of the engineer, and rode in style to the interior of Piedmont, one of the major maintenance installations on the railroad.

By the time reinforcements could arrive from the Federal post at nearby New Creek, the entire yard at Piedmont was in ruins. Several thousand feet of track had been torn from cross ties, and buildings, machine shops, and nine precious locomotives had been destroyed. McNeil's nearby rear guard had also managed to strike effectively by capturing and burning three additional trains and capturing one hundred men. It became

obvious to Kelley that McNeil had to be eliminated if the railroad was to be operated in safety.

If, as John Mosby stated, the value of a guerrilla could be measured by the number of men kept watching for him, Hanse McNeil was becoming invaluable to the Confederacy. The Federal War Department shortly ordered eleven regiments into positions along the B&O at a time when the Confederacy was seriously debating the usefulness of its Partisan Rangers and ordered all of them to disband. The order, however, exempted the

two most effective units that were operating in northern and northwestern Virginia: McNeil and Mosby would be allowed to remain in the field.

McNeil soon fell in combat and the source of the wound remains a Civil War mystery. In early October, he led an attack on a bridge near Mount Jackson and was mortally wounded by a shot that came from one of his own men, a guerrilla who had apparently been reprimanded for stealing chickens. But George Valentine, the man who did the shooting, may have had a different motivation than revenge over the dressing-down he received for chicken theft.

Hanse McNeil, like many of the other effective Confederate commanders, led his men by example as well as by orders, and was in the front of the attack at Mount Jackson when he was killed. Valentine shot him from the rear and fled the scene. Later, Valentine was identified as a Jessie Scout, a fact that leaves only two possibilities. One, Valentine shot McNeil and deserted to Sheridan's Shenandoah army to gain some degree of safety and volunteered to serve as a Jessie Scout. Sheridan had several deserters from the Confederate army within his "scout battalion." Two, there is an excellent chance that George Valentine, actually a Jessie Scout at the time of the shooting, had enrolled as a Partisan Ranger and rode with McNeil until he had an opportunity to kill him. McNeil had become a serious problem for the Federal commanders to manage and he had to be eliminated—through one method or another—and it is entirely plausible that an operation designed to kill the partisan leader had been developed within Sheridan's headquarters.

Having lost a key commander, the Confederate command turned to Harry Gilmor, a Baltimore native who was quite familiar with railroad operations. After blocking the tracks of the ever-threatened B&O in early 1864, Gilmor's raiders boarded the train and robbed the passengers at gunpoint, collecting pistols, watches, coats, and money. After another robbery, Gilmor was ordered before a court-martial, and though he returned to duty, the actions of Gilmor and his men resulted in the decision of the Confederate Congress to disband its partisans. With the killing of Hanse McNeil, the obvious choice of commander for McNeil's and Woodson's partisans was Harry Gilmor.

It was, however, the Jessie Scouts—now assigned under the command of Philip Sheridan—and their new commander, Major

Major Harry Gilmor was a cool, dashing, and reckless Confederate cavalry officer who represented the last connection between the Confederacy and Maryland. Once Brigadier General Bradley Johnson had been assigned to command a prisoner-of-war camp, Gilmor became the only prominent Marylander left in the Confederate army. This fact, his knowledge of Jessie Scout operations, and his new assignment as a threat to the Baltimore and Ohio Railroad made him a primary target.

General Philip Sheridan was the answer Lincoln and Grant had been seeking to eliminate the Confederate threat to Maryland, Pennsylvania, and Washington, D.C. Soon after he was given command, Sheridan defeated Jubal Early at Winchester in late summer 1864. His next major objective was to eliminate the Confederate raiders operating near his base areas. Gilmor was near the top of his list.

Henry Young, who would have the responsibility of bringing Gilmor and his raiders under control. Curiously, the operation that took shape inside Sheridan's headquarters closely resembled one of the explanations for Valentine's act against McNeil.

Small, highly mobile, two-man Jessie Scout teams were sent into Hardy County, Virginia, in an attempt to locate Gilmor. A second, larger team of scouts—disguised in Confederate uniforms—prepared to ride behind Confederate lines to capture the new partisan commander. The final aspect of the plan involved experienced Federal cavalrymen, handpicked from several commands, who would arrive at the scene of Gilmor's capture and serve as security escorts. The entire Federal capture plan was far more detailed and involved than the hasty plan thrown together by Andrews, which had resulted in failure in Georgia in early 1862. Sophistication had entered into federal planning, and officers, men, and a female agent who were capable of carrying complex plans through to completion had been located by this point in the war. The problem was as old as the military itself: the target had to be located and its position fixed, and sufficient force had to be moved to the target's vicinity to eliminate it.

Youthful Archibald Rowand, one of Averell's former scouts, of the 1st West Virginia Cavalry, and another scout were selected to perform the reconnaissance inside the Confederate stronghold of Moorefield. Having been in the battle that destroyed much of McCausland's command after the burning of Chambersburg, Rowand was quite familiar with the region. He was well versed in the names of Confederate commanders and their units, and he had survived a hostile interrogation after being captured in his Confederate uniform as Averell maneuvered toward Lynchburg with Hunter. In short, Rowand was excellent at what he did.

John H. "Hanse" McNeil was a bold Confederate Partisan Ranger who had led numerous successful attacks against Union facilities associated with the critical Baltimore and Ohio Railroad. While leading an attack on a covered bridge at Mt. Jackson in October 1864, he was mortally wounded by one of his own men, George Valentine, who shot him in the back and who was later reported to be a Jessie Scout. Harry Gilmor replaced McNeil and soon was the target of the Jessie Scouts.

This was a major operation, and a second Jessie Scout team—composed of Nick Carlisle, a Virginian, and Sergeant Mullihan of the 17th Pennsylvania—was also sent into Moorefield to look for signs of Gilmor. Reports exist that Sheridan also sent an unnamed female agent into the Confederate stronghold as well. The Union commanders in the region were determined to remove Harry Gilmor before he began damaging them as McNeil had.

Rowand and his companion reported back to Sheridan's headquarters in Winchester on February 3, 1865, and the female agent confirmed their reports that Gilmor was in Moorefield on the following day. The first part of the operation was complete: Gilmor had been located.

A force of twenty Jessie Scouts was assembled quickly from the men at Sheridan's headquarters, and they prepared to ride on February 4. Rowand, now familiar with Moorefield, would lead the operation back in the capture attempt, even though he had just finished an exhausting fifty-eight-mile (93km) winter ride the previous day. A composite force of three hundred volunteer cavalrymen, under the command of Lieutenant Colonel E.J. Whitaker of the 1st Connecticut Cavalry, would form the security element for the entire operation.

The cavalry element of the raid would follow several miles in the rear of the disguised Jessie Scouts, giving the appearance that they were tracking the Confederates as they rode to sanctuary in Moorefield. The scouts told one of two stories when questioned along the route: they were responding to the call from Gilmor for additional recruits, or they were from the Lost River picket post and were delivering a warning to Gilmor about the approach of the Union cavalrymen. In either case, the presence of Whitaker and his men in their rear gave credibility to their stories.

Once the Jessie Scouts entered the town of Moorefield in the early-morning darkness of February 5, only a short time was needed to locate the house where Gilmor was staying. The Scouts' commander, Henry Young, and a few Jessies quietly climbed the stairs and entered the bedroom where Gilmor was sleeping. Contrary to the reports of several historians who have written that Gilmor was in bed with a woman, he was in fact sharing a bed with his cousin, Hoffman Gilmor, who was also captured. Gilmor wrote about his capture:

My cousin, H——— G———, was in bed with me, when the door suddenly opened, and five men with drawn pistols, and although dressed as Confederates, I saw at a glance what they were. But it was too late for a fight, for they had seized my pistols, lying on a chair under my uniform. "Are you Colonel Gilmor?" said one of them. I did not answer at first; I was glancing around to see if there was any chance of escape. My attention was arrested by feeling the muzzle of a pistol against my head, and hearing the question repeated. "Yes, and who in the Devil's name are you?" "Major Young, of General Sheridan's Staff." "All right. I suppose you want me to go with you?" "I shall be happy to have your company to Winchester, as General Sheridan wishes to consult with you about some important military matters."

The difficult portion of the operation was now to begin. Young and his men had secured their captive, but they were deep within Confederate-controlled territory and Gilmor's men were roused. Three made a sudden charge against the capture party as Gilmor was "introduced" to Whitaker, and the long ride back to Winchester began.

Whitaker placed a force of thirty-eight men, fifteen of whom were armed with Spencers, in the back of the column to act as a rear guard. They held off repeated Confederate advances and retained their prized prisoner before stopping for the night. During this stop, Gilmor reported that he was closely guarded by a man who had served in the Confederate army under him before deserting to the Union army. This Jessie Scout, a Confederate deserter dressed in a Confederate uniform, was taking enormous risks with his life: if captured in either uniform he would be hanged, either as a deserter or as a spy.

En route to Winchester and Sheridan, the Jessie Scouts encountered and captured another of their enemies, Captain George Stump, who was near his father's home on the Romney road. Several accounts exist about this event, but what is certain is that George Stump did not survive his meeting with the Jessie Scouts. According to one story, he was executed at the order of Young when it was determined that he was "too sick to ride," and Young ordered his scouts to "make him sicker." Another account, related by Rowand, tells that Stump refused to give his parole and attempted to snatch Young's pistol from its holster. Young had him shot to death for his efforts. A third report exists in which Young gave Stump an opportunity to ride swiftly away before his scouts opened fire, but Stump was killed as he departed. Regardless of the execution details, George Stump found little mercy at the hands of the Jessie Scouts that night near Romney. As guerilla fighters, the scouts expected no mercy if captured, and gave little to their enemies.

Harry Gilmor was delivered to General Sheridan in Winchester on Monday, February 6. There, he was confined in handcuffs to a small hotel room. The operation to secure Gilmor had begun on January 31, when

Rowand rode for Moorefield. Within a week, the Jessie Scouts had ridden 232 miles (373km) over bad mountain roads in the worst of deep winter conditions to deliver Gilmor to Winchester. Archibald Rowand wrote about the daring expedition in a letter to his father:

> ...our trip was a perfect success. Succeeded in capturing the notorious Harry Gilmor and fifteen men of different commands. On Tuesday I was ordered to go with one man to Moorefield. By the order of Gen. Sheridan, went to Moorefield and returned on Thursday, reported to the General the whereabouts of Harry Gilmor and command. The General requested me to send in a written report to be filed. On Saturday morning a force of cavalry (300) and twenty scouts left this place for Moorefield, distant fifty-eight miles [93km]. Traveling all night, we arrived at Moorefield Sunday morning just before day. Leaving the town surrounded by a strong picket, we struck the South Fork river road....
>
> Dashing across the fields, we surrounded the Williams' house and caught one of Rosser's men. Major Young went on to Randolph's and there caught Harry in bed. He was a little astonished, but took things coolly. You may be sure that we gave him no chance to escape.

Henry Halleck sent a telegram with directions for the imprisonment of Gilmor: "Major Gilmor will be sent to Fort Warren for confinement. A special guard will be selected to take him there." Sheridan's Jessie Scouts, including Major Young, personally escorted Gilmor to prison in Boston Harbor, allowing him no chance to escape.

Lieutenant Colonel Edward W. Whitaker led the Union extraction force that included men from his regiment, the 1st Connecticut Cavalry, during the Jessie Scout operation that netted Harry Gilmor for Sheridan. The hazardous mission, fifty-eight miles (93 km) deep inside Confederate territory, was achieved without serious losses to the Union cavalrymen.

JESSIE SCOUTS CAPTURE HARRY GILMOR

A Prisoner and His Captor

Harry Gilmor was one of the few Civil War soldiers who later wrote about his own wartime capture. The Confederate soldier and his captor, Major Henry Young of Sheridan's Union scouts, quickly developed a bond verging on actual friendship that was based on their mutual respect for each other's courage and character.

Gilmor wrote about those cold February days:

I had not gone half a mile [0.8km] before Major Young thought it best to put me on a more indifferent horse, saying, "Colonel, I can not trust you on such a splendid animal, for you know that you will leave us if you get the smallest chance." He was right, for I was already on the look-out for a break in the fence to make the effort.

My feelings can not be imagined as I passed through Moorefield, and saw the ladies run out into the street—some of them weeping—to bid me good-by, and express their sorrow for my situation. I tried to be cheerful, but it was hard to bear.

Major Gilmor was extremely proud of his service to the Confederacy and posed for this post-war photograph after he had regained all of the weight he had lost while a prisoner of war in Boston Harbor. His officer's jacket was too tight to be buttoned for the portrait session.

We took the river road to Romney, to get on the Northwestern Turnpike to Winchester. H—— [Hoffman, Gilmor's cousin] and I rode at the head of the column with Colonel Whittington [Whitaker], while some of the other prisoners were kept in the centre by the provost guard. These prisoners were about a dozen or so of Rosser's and Imboden's men, picked up by them as they had gone along.

Night came on soon after leaving Romney, and, though the weather was intensely cold, and the horses very tired, we pushed on six or seven miles [10–11km] farther, when we halted for an hour to refresh both man and horse. The colonel, Major Young, the surgeon (Dr. Walls), H——, and I, with a guard of about ten men of the squad, went to a house near by for supper, and then we continued on our way to Winchester.

The night was so very cold that most of us had to dismount and walk. In passing through the mountain, I watched closely for an opportunity of breaking away and plunging down the steep hill-side; but four men were constantly near me with pistols drawn and cocked, and no chance appeared until we got within two or three miles [3–4km] of Big Capon River. Here Major Young asked the colonel to turn me over to him, and let him push rapidly ahead to Winchester; but the colonel refused, and the Major, becoming angry, took all his men, the scouts, off with him to Winchester. These were the only men I cared for, and I felt certain now of making my escape.

We were then some distance ahead of the main column, and when Young and his men left us there were none in sight except the colonel and his orderly, the surgeon, H——, and myself. We halted, and the orderly was sent back to hurry up a fresh guard for me. The doctor and H—— were on their horses, while the colonel and I were standing in the road in advance of them. The place, too, was a good one, on the side of a small mountain, and I made up my mind to seize the colonel before he could draw his pistol, throw him down, and make my escape. I was then about three paces from him when I formed this plan, had moved up closer to carry it into effect, and was just about to make the spring, when I was seized with an unacountable fit of trembling, and could not move. It was not fear, for although the colonel was even a larger man than myself, powerfully made, and apparently a cool head, I knew that my success was certain; for who could stand such a sudden shock as he would certainly have received? I had been standing there for some time, and was very cold, but I never trembled like that except when I had an ague-chill. I can not account for it; all I know is, that to keep him from noticing it, and not dreaming that any of his scouts would return, I put my hand on H——'s horse, and at length quieted my nerves, when suddenly up dashed four scouts. The snow was so deep they gave no sound of their approach. They had been sent back by Major Young for my guard. My heart sank within me; but I determined not to enter Winchester without making a strong effort to escape....We reached Winchester about noon, when I was separated from the other prisoners and taken to a small room in the hotel, destitute of furniture except a chair and the frame of an old bedstead. It was severely cold, but I was allowed no fire. Two sentinels, kept in the room, were instructed by the lieutenant to shoot me if I passed a line chalked on the floor.

The lieutenant gave me a pair of his own blankets, or I would have had none, for I gave mine to H——. I asked the provost marshall for something to lie upon, but he sent, instead, handcuffs. A number were brought before a pair of the "ruffles," as they were called then, was found to fit, and for the first time, I found myself in irons. I asked by whose authority I was subjected to this indignity, and was told that it was by the order of General Sheridan. I knew it was useless to appeal to him, and so spent an hour in cursing the crew, and wound up by flinging in a few lively epithets at the head of the guard, rather ungenerously, for it seems they were ordered to hold no conversation with me, and consequently could not reply.

One of the scouts (White), a decent, brave man, brought me every day a glass of toddy; but apart from this, I had only common army rations. I was allowed to see no one, although several ladies went to Sheridan and begged to be permitted to visit me. . . .

On the morning of the third day Major Young informed me that I was to be taken to some other prison, but he would not tell me where. The irons being removed, I found about twenty-five cavalry-men ready to escort me to Stevenson's Depot, where I was to take the cars to Harper's [sic] Ferry. Major Young had seven or eight of his scouts with him, and informed me that they would accompany me to the fort where I was to be confined. I guessed at once that Fort Warren was to be my prison, and, not long after, the major con-firmed my suspicion. From first to last, he was as kind to me as it was possible for him to be, but, at the same

time, he watched me like a hawk, and was always ready to draw his revolver. He told me frankly that he would not trust me far, for he knew that I would take desperate chances to escape. He did not iron me, as he had been ordered, nor did he ask me for my parole of honor, but I did not make a movement that was not quickly seen.

On arriving at Harper's Ferry, we had some difficulty in getting through the crowd assem-bled to meet us, and at one time it looked rather squally, for they threat-ened me with violence. Major Young, perfectly cool, waved them aside with his pistol at full cock, and whispered to me, in event of attack, to take one of his pistols and shoot right and left. "They will have," said he, "to walk over my dead body before they touch you." The cow-ardly scoundrels made a good deal of noise, but, finding they made no impression, began to slink off, when a tall, vulgar-looking lieutenant of artillery, somewhat intoxi-cated, cried out at the top of his voice, "I say, Gilmor, where is the watch some of

your thieves stole from me on the Philadelphia train?"

Without deigning to utter a syllable, Major Young gave him a power-ful blow across the mouth with the barrel of his pis-tol, which knocked him from the low platform. The fellow got up, with blood streaming out, and slunk off without another word. This stopped all the talk about taking me from Major Young . . . we left in the cars, reached New York the same evening, traveled all that night, and arrived in Boston at 7 A.M. on the 10th of February, 1865.

The major escorted me to the United States Hotel, where I should have enjoyed a good breakfast but for the crowd of men and women huddled together, gazing at me from every direction.

Major Young kindly accompanied me about town to make some pur-chases, and then conduct-ed me to my prison home. Its gates closed upon me, and I had struck my last blow for the South. Though fully entitled to my exchange as a regularly commissioned officer, it was soon quite apparent

that the government designed, if possible, to keep me back among those from whom this right was to be arbitrarily withheld. . . . and, at length, on the 24th of July, 1865, the action of the President on officers of my rank brought the order with which my captivity was to end, and having complied with the regulations pre-scribed, I was paroled and released on that day.

Major Henry Harrison Young returned to duty as chief of Sheridan's scouts, and by the time Gilmor was released, had been sent to Texas with Sheridan and four (or possibly six) of his scouts, a group that included the brave man who provided Gilmor with a daily "toddy"—Sergeant Jim White.

They were ordered into Mexico—wearing their old Confederate uniforms—to col-lect information on the status of the Confederate soldiers who escaped across the international border to the French, Austrian, and Belgian army units that were supporting Emperor Maximilian and the Imperial Mexican army. Young was Sheridan's go-between with the camp of Benito Juarez and his Liberal army seeking to over-throw Maximilian, and several trips were made into northern

Mexico by the Union officer and his scouts. At one time, Young, Sheridan, and Grant in Washington discussed a plan to abduct the imperial garrison commander in Matamoros, Mexico, much like they had done with Gilmor.

Young was reported killed while leading a river crossing at the Rio Grande in late 1866 and his body was never recovered for burial. It was left to Jim White to complete the final mission of Sheridan's scouts.

Once Maximilian had been captured, he was tried by Juarez's officers at Querétaro, a city located 100 miles [161km] north of Mexico City. The former emperor was condemned

to death by firing squad—as he had done with many of his captives—and Secretary of State Seward, in Washington, began to receive pleas from European governments to intercede on their behalf to save his life.

Seward had no representative in Mexico, as the "Minister to Mexico" was located in New Orleans where he remained in contact with Juarez's officers. Having no way to deliver a diplomatic note deep within the interior of central Mexico, Seward or his minister requested assistance from Sheridan's headquarters and Sheridan called for Sergeant Jim White.

White was sent across the Gulf of Mexico on the steamer *The Black Bird,* and after landing at Tampico, he rode on horseback across Mexico, possibly still wearing the old Confederate uniform the scouts had used as disguises during the Civil War, and delivered Seward's message. Unfortunately for Maximilian, the request for mercy had no effect on Juarez's generals and the emperor was executed.

White was just as he was described by Harry Gilmor, "a brave, decent man" who risked his life for his country long after the Civil War was over. He delivered his message to Querétaro in early 1867—completing the last mission of Sheridan's scouts.

Major Henry Harrison Young served bravely with the 2nd Rhode Island Infantry Regiment, but the life of an infantry officer was too routine for him. His talents as a scout were discovered by Sheridan, who made him his assistant aide-de-camp and chief scout. Young led the deep penetration raid that resulted in the capture of Harry Gilmor, later captured Brigadier General Felix Barringer, and accompanied Sheridan to Texas at the end of hostilities with a few of his scouts—including Arch Rowand. Young died in Mexico in November 1866, while on a mission for Sheridan, but his service record describes a retroactive mustering out of service— back to July 15, 1865. His service in Mexico, which cost him his life, was classified secret by the army.

chapter

9

JOHN YATES BEALL'S MARITIME RAID

> "Nor must Uncle Sam's web-feet be forgotten. At all the watery margins they have been present. Not only the deep sea, the broad bay, and the rapid river, but also up the muddy bayou, and where the ground was a little damp, they have been and made their tracks."
>
> —Abraham Lincoln

The United States was developing into a powerful commercial maritime force on the world stage. Large numbers of ships carrying the freight and raw materials necessary to keep the war machine well oiled sailed the world's oceans. The Federal navy was sufficiently strong, relative to their Confederate opponent, in the initial stages of the war to begin the imposition of a blockade that was designed to bring the South to its knees through economic deprivation. Primarily agricultural, the Southern economy depended heavily on imports of manufactured goods from the North and Europe. Trade was necessary for the survival of the South and the access to trade was blocked. This was something that would not go unchallenged by the Confederacy. Raiders soon went to sea, and other operations were also under way.

One of the raiders who was less well known than some of the Confederates who covered the wide oceans as commerce raiders and nearly wrecked the Union's maritime industry was John Yates Beall, a former infantryman who had served in the Stonewall Brigade and been severely wounded.

Soon after recovering, he served the Confederacy as a secret agent in Iowa. Fearing that he would be discovered, he fled to Canada. He quickly contacted the Confederate government's representatives as he began to develop a plan for a stunning raid on Federal interests.

Lying in Sandusky Bay on Lake Erie was Johnson's Island, now used by the Federal authorities as a prison for Confederate officers who fell into their hands. Beall thought that a raid on the island to free the prisoners

JOHN YATES BEALL'S MARITIME RAID

110

PAGE 111: Johnson's Island was a Federal prison camp located in Sandusky Bay in Lake Erie. The location was far too cold for the Southerners, and forty-nine of the Confederate officers held captive there froze to death during a single January night. ABOVE: Although Union soldiers died of disease and starvation in Southern prison camps, there was no actual intent to place them under conditions that were unsanitary or to deprive them of food. In most cases, Union prisoners received essentially the same rations given to Confederate soldiers. In the North, however, things were different. At Johnson's Island, officer-prisoners organized rat hunts to find food.

and set them loose in Ohio would tie down large numbers of Union troops. The troops would attempt to recapture the prisoners, preventing them from joining in the fight against the Confederacy. Beall traveled to Richmond and discussed his proposal in person with Stephen R. Mallory, the Confederate secretary of the navy.

Secretary Mallory thought the plan feasible but doubted that it could be carried out from neutral Canada without damaging the

Confederacy's relationship with Great Britain. He suggested an alternative: privateering in the shipping lanes of the Chesapeake Bay. The suggestion led to a commission for Beall in the Confederate navy. He was now an "acting master," and was given a few pistols and swords. Beall was required by the commission to recruit his own men, but they couldn't be subject to military service, and as privateers they would have no salary and would be dependent on the "prizes" they

captured for their pay. Privateering so closely resembled open piracy that it had been outlawed by most of the seafaring nations. Those undertaking it knew they could expect harsh penalties if captured.

This, of course, didn't deter Beall, and he recruited a lieutenant, Bennett G. Burleigh, and other men who would participate in several successful attacks in the Chesapeake Bay region in 1863. His raids included cutting the cable to the eastern shore and destroying the Federal lighthouse near Cape Charles. After capturing two small open boats, the seaborne guerrillas began to raid in earnest. In a short time, Beall and his men had captured and destroyed a dozen ships with their own two. They captured a large sloop loaded with sutler supplies for the Federal garrison at Port Royal, South Carolina, and attempted to run the blockade in order to sell the prized booty in Richmond. Unfortunately for the privateers, a Federal gunboat fired on them, setting fire to the ship. Although they lost most of the cargo, they escaped capture until the Union authorities ordered three infantry regiments, an artillery battalion, and ten gunboats into the Chesapeake—a massive force to stop the "pirates."

They were soon captured and sent in chains to Fort McHenry, where they were tried as pirates. They would have been hanged except for the intervention of the Richmond authorities, who placed an equal number of captured Union soldiers and officers in chains and threatened to give them the same treatment that was given to the captured privateers. Washington, under the threat of retaliation, held them as ordinary prisoners of war and exchanged them on May 5, 1864.

Beall went directly to Richmond to review his old plan for action on the Great Lakes with the Confederate authorities. By 1864 the end for the Confederacy was much

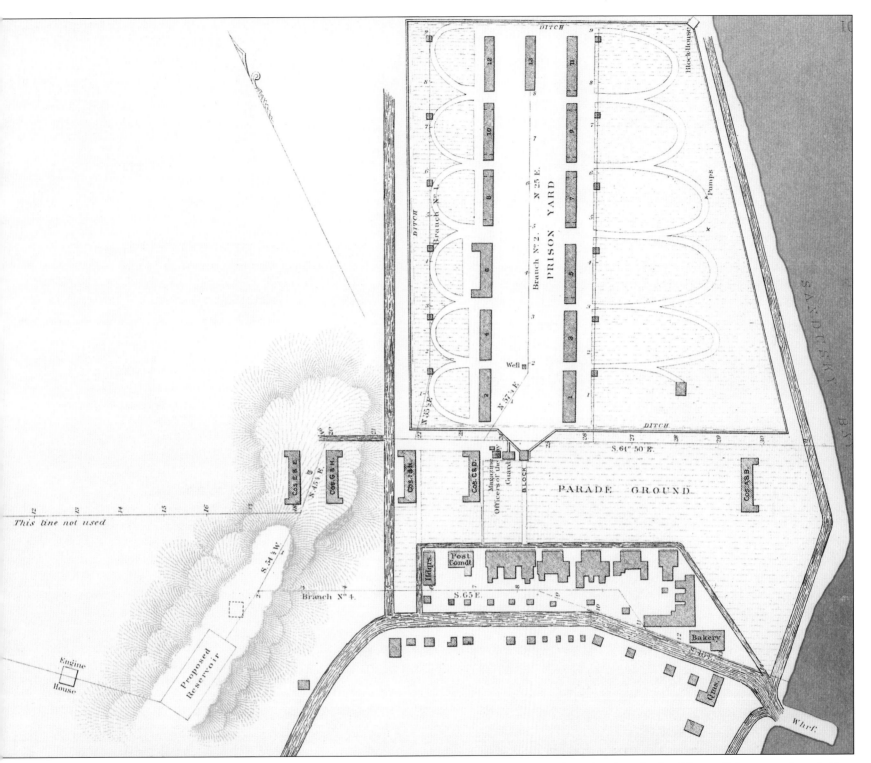

The prison camp at Johnson's Island was well organized, but because it lay within a deep bay, Beall's raiders hoped to be able to sail close enough to shell the Union guards and permit a mass escape.

JOHN YATES BEALL'S MARITIME RAID

Prison guards, both Union and Confederate, were under orders to fire at any prisoner who stepped across a marked "dead line." Federal guards were ordered to fire at any exposed light within a barracks after "lights out," and many prisoners lost their lives to shots fired suddenly through barracks windows.

seemed more appropriate to the officers in the Southern government. The letter contained instructions for Dahlgren to kill Jefferson Davis and other members of the Confederate government. Real or fraudulent, the letter was accepted at face value by many Confederates, and clandestine projects were approved more quickly than ever before. Beall's plan was ratified and he was once again off to Canada.

He envisioned a full campaign on Lake Erie. First, he proposed to capture the USS *Michigan,* a fourteen-gun warship—the only warship allowed by a treaty on the lake. Once the *Michigan* was in his possession, the lake cities would become easy prey for his men to attack as they pleased. The destruction being felt by the South would be felt in the far North.

The second phase of the campaign involved a raid on the original target in Beall's plan: the prison on Johnson's Island. Due to the captured warship, there would be little opposition. Once the prisoners (all officers) were set free, local Copperheads—Northerners who supported the South—would provide them with mounts and arms, and they could flee toward the safety of Virginia by passing through the new state of West Virginia. Beall and his men would then be able to steam at will on Lake Erie and shell Sandusky, Cleveland, and Buffalo if they chose to do so.

Burleigh, his old lieutenant from the Chesapeake raiding days, was the first to join Beall in the new venture, and together they located additional men from Confederate sympathizers and escaped prisoners who had found refuge in Canada. One of the Confederate commissioners in Canada, Jacob Thompson—the recent secretary of the interior under Buchanan—was the primary secret agent of the Confederacy in Canada, and he identified an agent of his who would prove useful as the plan developed.

more apparent and many similar operations began to be acceptable to the government. Following the discovery of a revealing letter on the body of Union officer Ulric Dahlgren, who was killed on a raid against Richmond, unconventional operations against the North

"War is cruelty and you cannot refine it."

—General William T. Sherman

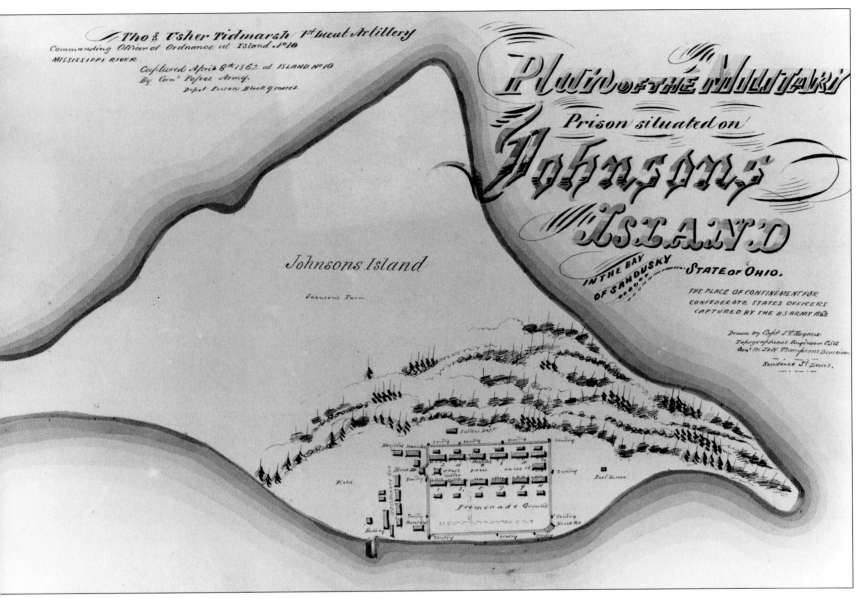

Johnson's Island was an ideal prison. Surrounded by water, there was little that escaped prisoners could do once they had eluded their guards. Many attempts were made, including that of a few brave souls who tried to walk across the frozen lake to reach Canada, but few men were able to get off of Johnson's Island without being exchanged.

Captain Charles H. Cole, a former member of Nathan Bedford Forrest's command, had been living in a hotel in Sandusky, posing as a wealthy young man from Philadelphia. He had spent freely, made friends with the officers guarding the prisoners on Johnson's Island, and developed good relations with the officers assigned to the *Michigan*. Like any good friend, he had been taken on tours of the ship and the prison where he had used money to recruit assistants for his espionage activities. Thompson was right: this man would be very useful to the plot to take control of Lake Erie.

Cole planned a great party at his hotel—to be held while the ship's captain and a group of his agents were away—and invited all of his Federal friends. Those Union officers not drunk would be drugged. Once this was accomplished, Cole was to fire a flare to signal Beall and the prisoners on the island

U.S.S. WOLVERINE (FORMERLY U.S.S. MICHIGAN.)
OLDEST IRON GUN BOAT IN THE WORLD, BUILT IN 1843.

Kind regards to major and
Yours 6th RSM —

The USS Michigan was the only warship permitted on Lake Erie by an international treaty. Beall's plan included its capture, after which they would sail it to shell Johnson's Island before moving on to shell both Sandusky and Cleveland, Ohio.

that the officers were under his control. At that point, Beall would move with his men to take over the *Michigan* and fire a shell into the island's officer's quarters. The twenty-five hundred prisoners would move against their surprised guards, who had few officers to direct a response. It was a good plan with a high probability of success.

The raid began to unfold gradually as the steam ferry *Philo Parsons* departed from Detroit on her daily run to Sandusky. One of her passengers that day was Burleigh, and

when the ferry docked briefly at Sandwich, on the Canadian side of the lake, Beall and two others came aboard. Later, at Amherstburg, sixteen other raiders boarded with a large trunk as their only piece of baggage. At about 5:00 P.M., after the *Philo Parsons* made its last stop before arriving in Sandusky, the disguised Confederates made their first move. Beall held a pistol at the head of the ferry's helmsman while Burleigh and the others herded the frightened passengers into rooms.

The ferry was landed at an island to take on wood and prisoners when they saw a second ferry, the *Island Queen,* approach. Beall and a few others leaped aboard from the upper deck of the *Philo Parsons*. Soon, shots were fired, the engineer of the *Island Queen* was wounded, and the second ferry was held by the Confederate raiders. The raiders were now within ten miles (16km) of the *Michigan* and all eyes strained to locate the signal flare to be fired by Captain Cole when the Union officers at his party were under his control.

The *Island Queen* was taken into deep water and allowed to sink slowly as the raiders cleared the decks of the *Philo Parsons* for action. Freight was thrown overboard as the ferry quietly slipped closer to Sandusky and the *Michigan*. As the warship's lights came into view, everyone began to realize that the signal from Cole was long overdue and the nearly foolproof operation was in danger of premature discovery.

Shortly afterward, the Confederate crewmen mutinied, refusing to go forward against a warship that might have learned of their approach. Only Beall, Burleigh, and one of the crew were willing to continue. Beall forced each of the men to sign a declaration that they would not continue before he reversed his course, admitting to himself that his long-hoped-for raid had failed.

Cole, one of Thompson's best agents, had been exposed. The captain of the *Michigan* had returned to the ship one day earlier than planned and had received a telegram from Detroit that explained the entire plot. Cole had been arrested.

In custody and facing capital charges for espionage, Cole quickly became an informer and exposed everyone involved. Arrests were swift, and the plot, only recently felt to be foolproof, had fallen to pieces.

Beall continued to attempt sabotage operations from Canada. He was arrested on December 16, 1864, when his team attempted to derail a train. He was tried as a spy by a military commission at Fort Lafayette. Found guilty, he was sentenced to death and hanged on Governor's Island in New York Harbor on February 24, 1865.

John Beall had attempted to bring the Civil War to a population that had been insulated from the destruction and violence seen throughout the South, particularly in his native Virginia. Had Charles Cole been able to gain control of the officers who were invited to attend his party in Sandusky, the outcome might have been quite different, and the single warship allowed on Lake Erie could have devastated important Federal and state military and industrial facilities along the lakeshore. This strong blow for the Confederacy against the Union would have occurred in September 1864, just two months prior to the general election in which Lincoln would face McClellan, a peace candidate. The presence of the Confederate navy on Lake Erie would have certainly been on the minds of many voters as they made their final decision within the privacy of the poll booth.

Unbelievable suffering occurred at Johnson's Island during the terrible winters. These men are walking beside the prison's dead line during a winter storm that left even the men inside their barracks freezing.

The Controversial Raid on Richmond

A report prepared by a secret agent working for the Union army may have sparked one of the most controversial operations of the Civil War—one that would have ramifications far beyond the battlefield. Joseph H. Maddox had reported that Richmond was nearly defenseless, and that one or two thousand cavalrymen "could land on the Pamunkey at dark and ride in unmolested and take Davis." While the report would be widely ignored, by February 1864, it seems that one man took it seriously and prepared to take advantage of the reported weakness in Richmond's defenses.

The winter fighting season had come to an end when the new commander of the Army of the Potomac and victor at Gettysburg, General George Meade, ordered his army to move north of the Rapidan River and enter winter quarters in the vicinity of Culpeper, Virginia. It was during this period that a brigadier general named Judson Kilpatrick, a cavalry commander in the Army of the Potomac, was able to gain the ear—temporarily—of Abraham Lincoln.

Kilpatrick managed to convince Lincoln that a division-sized raid into Richmond was entirely feasible, and the president approved the plan; General Meade seems to have grudgingly agreed. Before long, Kilpatrick was prepared to move, and a flurry of orders and reports began to flow from the Union commander's headquarters. One announced the contemplated move:

February 28, 1864.
Major-General WARREN,
Commanding Second
Corps:

The major-general commanding directs me to inform you that General Kilpatrick will move to-night, cross the Rapidan at the lower fords, and turning the enemy's right flank operate in his rear. He will be absent several days. He will withdraw all the supports and reserves of his picket-line, but will leave his pickets.

Another dispatch advised the overall army commander, Henry Halleck, of the planned move and asked that General Benjamin Butler, commanding an army near Fort Monroe, be advised that Kilpatrick could arrive there without announcement as he withdrew from the vicinity of Richmond.

February 29, 1864—10
A.M.
(Received 11.30 A.M.)

Maj. Gen. H.W. HALLECK,
General-in-Chief:

A cavalry expedition left last evening with the intention of attempting to carry Richmond by a coup de main, General Kilpatrick in command. If successful, expects to be there by tomorrow P.M., March 1, and may the next day be in the vicinity of General Butler's outposts and pickets. Will you please notify that officer, that his advanced posts may be warned?

GEO. G. MEADE

Judson Kilpatrick had proposed to capture Richmond by a surprise attack with his small but highly mobile force as he freed the estimated fifteen thousand prisoners of war believed to be held in the immediate area of the Confederate capital. As part of the agreement he had made with Lincoln, Kilpatrick promised to distribute thousands of leaflets promising a general amnesty to those Virginians who were willing to take an oath of allegiance to the Federal government.

On the night of February 28, 1864, Kilpatrick's thirty-five hundred men recrossed the Rapidan River and rode south, hoping to be in and out of Richmond before the Confederate army could react to their presence. At Spotsylvania Court House, Kilpatrick split his force, sending a separate five-hundred man force under the command of Colonel Ulric Dahlgren in a wide swing to the west.

It was this portion of the raid that created a controversy that is still argued over today. Colonel Dahlgren was the son of Rear Admiral John Dahlgren, the inventor of the heavy and much-used Dahlgren gun. Ulric Dahlgren was only twenty-one years old—among the youngest colonels in the Union army—and he was on the operation in spite of the loss of one of his legs in fighting at Hagerstown at the end of the Gettysburg campaign. His part of the raid was complex: he was to ride to the south of Richmond, enter the city, and free the prisoners while Kilpatrick rode against the city's northern defenses and drew the Confederate reserves toward the main force.

At first, the raid went according to plan. Kilpatrick pushed his force all through the first night and the following day as the weather changed for the worse. Exhausted horses fell and never rose as the commander known to his men as "Kill Cavalry" began to live up to his name.

The Union cavalrymen stopped just short of

Richmond's defenses on March 1, but there was no sign that Dahlgren had entered the city as he had been instructed before he rode away from the main column at Spotsylvania Court House. The Union soldiers continued to skirmish with the Confederate defenders for most of the day as they waited for the arrival of Dahlgren's small column, but there was no sign of them, so Kilpatrick withdrew his men a few miles and set up a temporary camp. Confederate pursuers, under General Wade Hampton, arrived during the night and began to drop artillery rounds into Kilpatrick's camp. The Union cavalrymen withdrew even farther from the city as they were fired on by Hampton's men, but there was still no word on the fate of Dahlgren. The mystery was soon resolved as three hundred of Dahlgren's men rode into Kilpatrick's temporary camp. One of the officers who rode with Dahlgren reported:

We left division headquarters at Stevensburg, Va., at 6 P.M. February 28, 1864, and marched to Ely's Ford, which we reached about 11 P.M. We crossed the river, and a party of the Fifth New York Cavalry, under Lieutenant Merritt, and Hogan, the scout, captured the

Ulric Dahlgren, the son of Rear Admiral John Dahlgren, was one of the youngest colonels in the Union army. He lost a leg due to wounds suffered at Hagerstown during the final stages of the Gettysburg campaign, but this injury didn't stop him from leading his cavalrymen. He was killed in a raid that may have been intended to decapitate the Confederacy of its leadership.

enemy's picket-post, 1 officer and 14 men, belonging to a North Carolina regiment of cavalry. The colonel then pressed on to Spotsylvania Court-House, which he reached at early dawn on the 29th February, marched on in the direction of Frederick's Hall till 8 A.M., when he halted for fifteen minutes to feed the horses; then

pressed on again to within three-fourths of a mile [1.2km] of Frederick's Hall Station, which we reached about 11 A.M.

On the road we captured 16 artillery soldiers belonging to the Maryland Battalion. They told us that at the station there were three different camps, eight batteries in each, in all about ninety-

six guns; that there was a regiment of infantry near at hand and a battalion of sharpshooters in each camp. Here we captured also 12 artillery officers on court-martial—1 colonel, 1 major, and 8 or 9 captains. What information they gave to Colonel Dahlgren I am unable to state, but he determined not to attack the camp and moved around them, cutting the railroad and telegraph about 1 mile [1.6km] south of the station.

We now pushed on to the South Anna, which we crossed about 10 o'clock on the night of the 29th instant. It was raining and so intensely dark that it was almost impossible to keep the column closed up, and some 50 men were lost in the darkness, but joined us again in the morning near Goochland Court-House. About 2 a.m. the colonel halted. The name of the place I am unable to state, but think it was about 9 miles [14.5km] from Goochland. At daylight of the morning of the 1st of March we marched on toward the James River and stopped for a few minutes near Horton's house, on the

JOHN YATES BEALL'S MARITIME RAID

canal, about 21 miles [46.7km] from Richmond. Here Colonel Dahlgren gave me orders to take the detachment (100 men) of the Second New York Cavalry, the ambulances, prisoners, led horses, [etc.], and proceed down the canal, destroying locks, burning mills, canal-boats, and all the grain I could find; that when I came to Westham Creek I should send the ambulances, prisoners, [etc.], under guard to Hungary Station, there to join General Kilpatrick and the main column; that I was then to proceed down the river road or the canal, as I might see fit, while he, with the main portion of his command, was to cross the James River at a ford which his guide was to show him, release the prisoners, and enter Richmond by, I believe, the Mayo Bridge. Here I was to join him, if possible; if not, make my way to Hungary Station and join General Kilpatrick. He then divided the torpedoes, giving me one box, some

Dahlgren (top row, third from right) with a group of officers in a photograph taken at Army of the Potomac headquarters, Falmouth, Virginia, in 1863.

turpentine and oakum. He then started ahead of me. I struck the canal and moved down along its bank, sending the ambulances, [etc.], under guard of Lieutenant Randolph and 20 men, on the river road, with orders to join me at Manakin's Bend. Along the canal I destroyed six flourishing grist-mills, filled with grain and flour, one saw-mill, six canal-boats, loaded with grain, the barn (also well filled) on Secretary Seddon's plantation, coal-works at Manakin's Ferry, and Morgan's Lock just above. Here I found that there were neither canal-boats, locks, nor mills on the canal till the Three-Mile Lock, i.e., 3 miles [4.8km] from Richmond. I could not bring the ambulances on the tow-path, so I took the river road again, reaching which I was surprised to find the tracks of Colonel Dahlgren's party, and farther on the dead body of a negro hanging from a tree on the roadside. It seems that Colonel Dahlgren intended to cross the James River by a ford, to which his guide (this negro) promised to guide him. There was nei-

ther ford nor bridge; the guide had known it, and in his indignation the colonel hung him.

Colonel Dahlgren, finding there was no way to cross the James save by a very small scow, abandoned the project and proceeded to the cross-roads, about 8 miles [13km] from Richmond, I think near Short Pump. Here I joined him about 3.30 P.M. He now sent off the ambulances, prisoners, led horses, [etc.], under guard and in charge of the signal officer. That is the last I saw of them....

...The movements of Colonel Dahlgren and Major Cooke, after our separation, are better known to you than to myself. With regard to the address and memoranda of plans alleged by rebel papers to have been found on Colonel Dahlgren's person, I would state that no address of any kind was ever published to either officers or men; that none of Colonel Dahlgren's plans, save what I have mentioned in the first part of my report, were ever made known to either officers or men in the expedition, and that I know it was not Colonel

Dahlgren's intention to kill Jeff. Davis, in case he could be captured. The following is a list of killed, wounded, and missing as accurately as I can get it: One officer killed, 4 officers missing, 194 enlisted men killed, wounded, and missing. Of this number about 60 are believed to be either killed or wounded.

Dahlgren had come quite close to Richmond before losing patience with his guide, Martin Robinson, and ordering him hanged. After the leading portion of his command became separated from the rest of his force, Dahlgren rode into an ambush that cost him his life. The ambush was reported by the officer who was in command of the Confederate force:

According to instructions I have the honor to report the facts concerning the little fight we had with the raiding party of the enemy around Richmond on the 5th day of March. I was informed by Lieutenant Pollard, of the Ninth Virginia Cavalry, that the enemy were advancing through King William County. I immediately ordered my men to report for duty, and succeeded in assembling 28 at King

and Queen Court-House. Lieutenant Pollard came up in their rear, and engaged their rear guard near Bruington Church, skirmishing for several miles. They halted and fed near Mantapike. The portions of the different commands were then collected together and put in ambush to await the advance of the enemy. After an hour or two's rest they moved on slowly. Our fire was reserved until the head of their column rested within a few yards, when they opened fire, which was instantly returned. Colonel Dahlgren fell dead, pierced with five balls. We captured 92 prisoners, 38 negroes, a number of horses, arms, [etc.]

Dahlgren was dead, his men killed, captured, or scattered. It was, however, not the audacity of the raid that created the controversy that survives to the present. When Dahlgren's body was searched, papers thought to be orders were found. These orders indicated that an escalation of this type of warfare was being considered by the Union army at this time.

Colonel Dahlgren had written to his father prior to the raid and, in part, the letter stated

In March 1864, General Lee left his temporary headquarters at Clark's Mountain to meet with Confederate President Jefferson Davis in Richmond. After the failed Federal raid, Lee returned to Clark's Mountain to prepare for a larger Federal advance.

JESSIE SCOUTS CAPTURE HARRY GILMOR

CONCLUSION

"Even the bravest cannot fight beyond his strength."

Homer, Iliad

Raids were a common strategy for those militarily weaker than their opponents, and an excellent tactic for the disadvantaged to use in circumstances under which they were unable to operate freely with regular formations. In the Civil War, the Confederates took advantage of this tactic more often—and more creatively—than the Union army.

Much like the operations of terrorists, raids leave the opponent off balance, with an implied threat of a repeat operation. The effect of a well-conducted raid is long-lasting, going beyond the single action, as defenders must carefully guard all potential targets, tying down enormous numbers of troops, while the raider has only to maneuver with a small group of fast-moving soldiers to be effective. In these scenarios, the raider has the advantage of being able to select from any number of lightly guarded or undefended targets while the defender must deploy forces futilely trying to protect everything.

Effective raids have a significant influence on morale, encouraging their own side, while unsettling the confidence of the army with the greater numbers. This was especially true during the last years of the Civil War, when half a nation struggled to preserve a way of life that would soon be history.

By planning small, strategic attacks, brave raiders like John S. Mosby had far greater impact on the war than their numbers would suggest.

BIBLIOGRAPHY

Beymer, William G. *On Hazardous Service*. New York: Harper and Brothers, 1912.

Brown, James E. "Life of Brigadier General John McCausland," *West Virginia History*, Vol. IV, No. 4, July 1943.

Early, Jubal; *Jubal Early's Memoirs,* Nautical and Aviation Publishing, Baltimore, 1989.

Gilmor, Harry. *Four Years in the Saddle. New York:* Harper and Brothers, 1866.

Hoke, J. *Reminiscences of the War*. Chambersburg, Pa.: privately printed, 1884.

Jones, Beuhring H. *The Sunny Land*. Baltimore: Innes and Company, 1868.

Lewis, Thomas. *The Shenandoah in Flames: The Valley Campaign of 1864.* Time-Life, 1987.

McCausland, John. "The Burning of Chambersburg," *Annals of the War, Written by Leading Participants, North and South.*Times Publishing, 1897.

Moore, Frank. The *Rebellion Record*. New York: G.P. Putnam, 1862.

O'Connor, Richard. *Sheridan, The Inevitable*. Indianapolis, In.: Bobbs-Merrill, 1953.

Reader, Frank S. *History of the Fifth West Virginia Cavalry*. New Brighton, Pa., 1890.

Sheridan, Philip H. *Personal Memoirs of P.H. Sheridan*. New York: Charles L. Webster and Company, 1888.

Stutler, Boyd B. *Civil War in West Virginia*. Charleston, WV: Educational Foundation, 1963.

Sutton, Joseph J. *History of the Second Regiment, West Virginia Volunteers, During the War of the Rebellion*. Portsmouth, Ohio, 1892.

Wallace, Lee. *A Guide to Virginia Military Organizations*. H.E. Howard, Inc., 1986.

War of the Rebellion, Official Records of the Union and Confederate Armies. 128 volumes.

PHOTO CREDITS

INDEX